Numbers to 20

Connect the dots.
Start at 1.

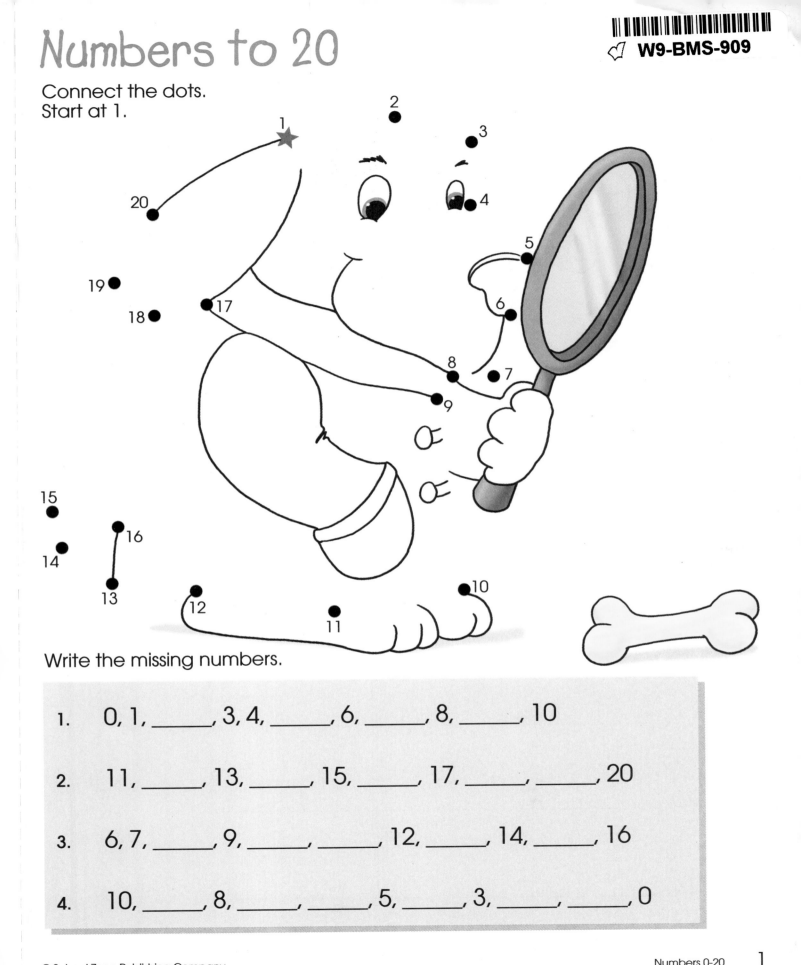

Write the missing numbers.

1.   0, 1, _____, 3, 4, _____, 6, _____, 8, _____, 10

2.   11, _____, 13, _____, 15, _____, 17, _____, _____, 20

3.   6, 7, _____, 9, _____, _____, 12, _____, 14, _____, 16

4.   10, _____, 8, _____, _____, 5, _____, 3, _____, _____, 0

W9-BMS-909

Numbers to 20

Find a path for the numbers 1-20 in order.
Start at 1.

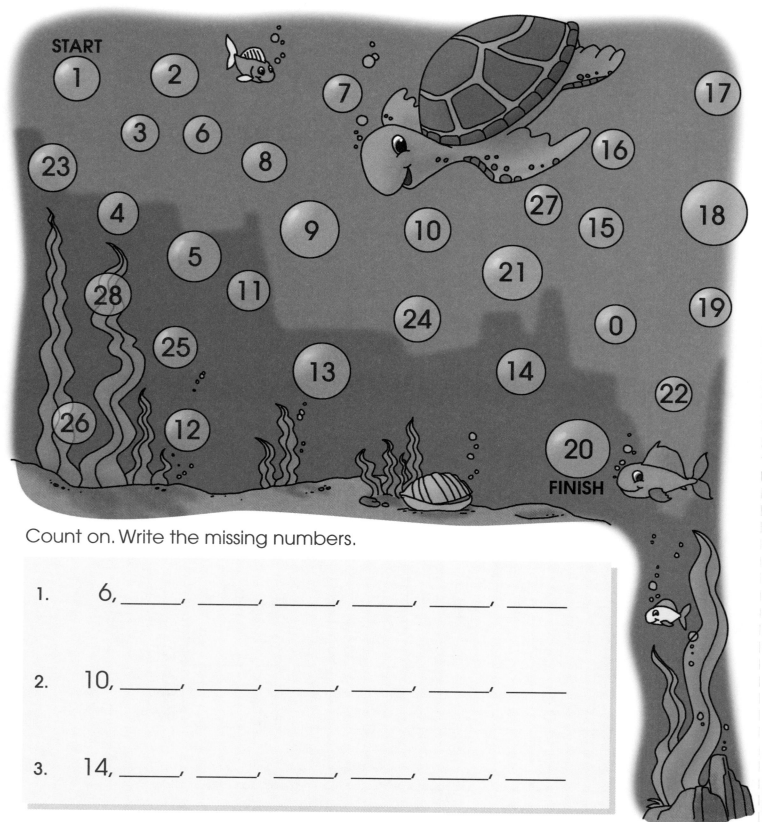

Count on. Write the missing numbers.

1. 6, _____, _____, _____, _____, _____

2. 10, _____, _____, _____, _____, _____

3. 14, _____, _____, _____, _____, _____

Before and After

Which number comes **before**?

1. _____ , 5   2. _____ , 9   3. _____ , 7

4. _____ , 3   5. _____ , 6   6. _____ , 11

7. _____ , 15   8. _____ , 17   9. _____ , 20

Which number comes **after**?

10. 6, _____   11. 2, _____   12. 7, _____

13. 11, _____   14. 9, _____   15. 15, _____

16. 13, _____   17. 19, _____   18. 17, _____

Before, Between, and After

before
$\underline{8}$, 9 , 10

8 , $\underline{9}$, 10
between

after
8 , 9 , $\underline{10}$

Which number comes **before**?

1. _____ , 6, 7   2. _____ , 10, 11   3. _____ , 14, 15

4. _____ , 11, 12   5. _____ , 18, 19   6. _____ , 1, 2

Which number belongs **between**?

7. 4, _____ , 6   8. 11, _____ , 13   9. 16, _____ , 18

10. 0, _____ , 2   11. 17, _____ , 19   12. 13, _____ , 15

Which number comes **after**?

13. 3, 4, _____   14. 15, 16, _____   15. 18, 19, _____

16. 6, 7, _____   17. 17, 18, _____   18. 8, 9, _____

Concepts of before, between, and after   © School Zone Publishing Company

Greater or Less

Greater means more than.
Less means not as many.

15
↑
greater

13
↑
less

Circle the number that is **greater**.

1. 5   8   2. 14   12   3. 19   9

4. 10   0   5. 2   12   6. 13   18

7. 13   3   8. 4   15   9. 20   12

Circle the number that is **less**.

10. 7   9   11. 11   8   12. 20   2

13. 15   11   14. 13   18   15. 0   3

16. 19   9   17. 17   19   18. 12   20

Concepts of *greater* and *less*

Greater Than or Less Than

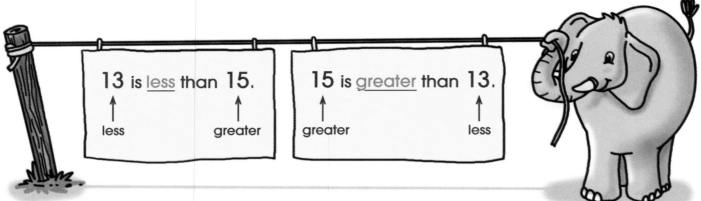

13 is <u>less</u> than 15.

↑ less   ↑ greater

15 is <u>greater</u> than 13.

↑ greater   ↑ less

Write the word **greater** or **less** in the blank.

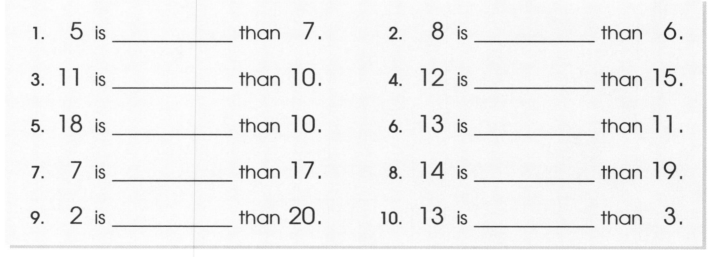

1. 5 is _____ than 7.
2. 8 is _____ than 6.
3. 11 is _____ than 10.
4. 12 is _____ than 15.
5. 18 is _____ than 10.
6. 13 is _____ than 11.
7. 7 is _____ than 17.
8. 14 is _____ than 19.
9. 2 is _____ than 20.
10. 13 is _____ than 3.

Write the correct number in the blank.

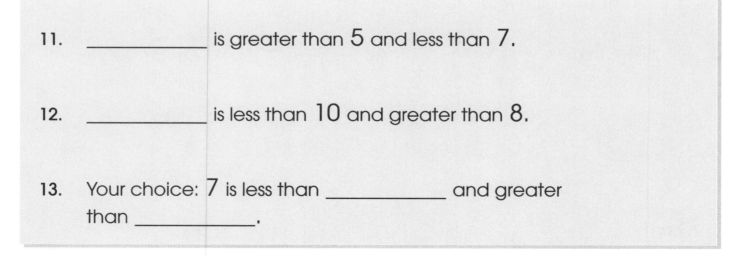

11. _____ is greater than 5 and less than 7.

12. _____ is less than 10 and greater than 8.

13. Your choice: 7 is less than _____ and greater than _____.

Sums through 10

The answer to an addition problem is called the **sum**.
You can write an addition number sentence like this: 3 + 4 = 7.

3 + 4 = _7_

Look at the picture. Read the number sentence.
Write the **sum**.

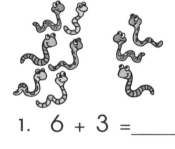

1. 6 + 3 = _____

2. 2 + 5 = _____

3. 8 + 0 = _____

4. 4 + 4 = _____

5. 5 + 4 = _____

6. 5 + 5 = _____

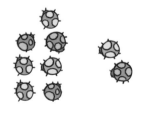

7. 7 + 2 = _____

8. 6 + 4 = _____

9. 8 + 2 = _____

10.

How many butterflies are there in all?   **9   10   11**

Write the number sentence.

_____

Addition facts; sums through 10   **7**

Sums of 10

The numbers you add are called **addends**.

Look at the picture. Read the number sentence.
Write the **sum** or missing **addend**.

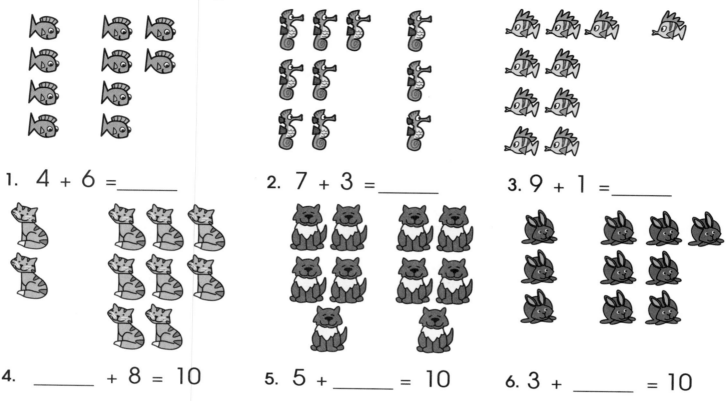

1. $4 + 6 =$ _____

2. $7 + 3 =$ _____

3. $9 + 1 =$ _____

4. _____ $+ 8 = 10$

5. $5 +$ _____ $= 10$

6. $3 +$ _____ $= 10$

7. Circle the pairs of numbers that make **sums** of 10.

4	5	5	2	3
1	6	8	4	7
9	3	7	4	6

8. **Challenge:** Circle two sets of three numbers (in rows or columns)
   that make **sums** of 10.

Find the Differences

The answer to a subtraction problem is called the **difference**.
You can write a subtraction number sentence like this: 11 - 4 = 7.

11 - 4 = _7_

Look at the picture. Read the number sentence.
Write the **difference**.

1.   7 - 3 = _____

2. 10 - 4 = _____

3. 10 - 8 = _____

4.   9 - 4 = _____

5.   9 - 7 = _____

6.   8 - 2 = _____

7.   7 - 4 = _____

8. 10 - 5 = _____

9.   8 - 3 = _____

10. How many more ducks
     than owls are there?   **4   5   6**

     Write the number sentence.

_____

Subtraction facts related to sums through 10

Subtraction Number Sentences

$9 - 3 = \underline{6}$

Look at the picture. Write the subtraction number sentence.

1. $6 - \underline{\hphantom{0}} = \underline{\hphantom{0}}$

2. $7 - \underline{\hphantom{0}} = \underline{\hphantom{0}}$

3. $\underline{\hphantom{0}} - 5 = \underline{\hphantom{0}}$

4. $\underline{\hphantom{0}} - \underline{\hphantom{0}} = \underline{\hphantom{0}}$

5. $\underline{\hphantom{0}} - \underline{\hphantom{0}} = \underline{\hphantom{0}}$

6. $\underline{\hphantom{0}} - \underline{\hphantom{0}} = \underline{\hphantom{0}}$

7. $\underline{\hphantom{0}} - \underline{\hphantom{0}} = \underline{\hphantom{0}}$

8. $\underline{\hphantom{0}} - \underline{\hphantom{0}} = \underline{\hphantom{0}}$

9. $\underline{\hphantom{0}} - \underline{\hphantom{0}} = \underline{\hphantom{0}}$

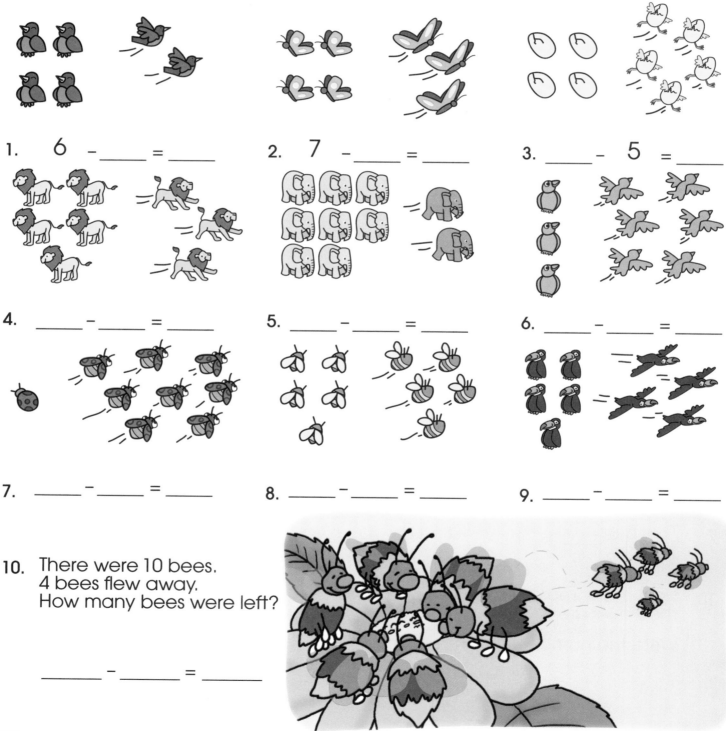

10. There were 10 bees.
4 bees flew away.
How many bees were left?

$\underline{\hphantom{000}} - \underline{\hphantom{000}} = \underline{\hphantom{000}}$

Subtraction facts related to sums through 10

Fact Families

A **fact family** uses the same numbers in its addition and subtraction problems.

$$
\begin{array}{r} 8 \\ + 4 \\ \hline 12 \end{array}
\quad
\begin{array}{r} 4 \\ + 8 \\ \hline 12 \end{array}
\quad
\begin{array}{r} 12 \\ - 4 \\ \hline 8 \end{array}
\quad
\begin{array}{r} 12 \\ - 8 \\ \hline 4 \end{array}
$$

Write the missing numbers to complete the **fact family**.

1.
$$
\begin{array}{r} 5 \\ + 7 \\ \hline \end{array}
\quad
\begin{array}{r} 7 \\ + 5 \\ \hline \end{array}
\quad
\begin{array}{r} 12 \\ - 5 \\ \hline \end{array}
\quad
\begin{array}{r} 12 \\ - 7 \\ \hline \end{array}
$$

2.
$$
\begin{array}{r} 5 \\ + 5 \\ \hline \end{array}
\quad
\begin{array}{r} 10 \\ - 5 \\ \hline \end{array}
$$

3.
$$
\begin{array}{r} \Box \\ + 6 \\ \hline 9 \end{array}
\quad
\begin{array}{r} 6 \\ + 3 \\ \hline \end{array}
\quad
\begin{array}{r} 9 \\ - \Box \\ \hline 3 \end{array}
\quad
\begin{array}{r} 9 \\ - 3 \\ \hline \end{array}
$$

4.
$$
\begin{array}{r} 6 \\ + \Box \\ \hline 12 \end{array}
\quad
\begin{array}{r} \Box \\ - 6 \\ \hline 6 \end{array}
$$

5.
$$
\begin{array}{r} 6 \\ + 5 \\ \hline \end{array}
\quad
\begin{array}{r} \Box \\ + 6 \\ \hline 11 \end{array}
\quad
\begin{array}{r} 11 \\ - \Box \\ \hline 6 \end{array}
\quad
\begin{array}{r} 11 \\ - \Box \\ \hline 5 \end{array}
$$

6.
$$
\begin{array}{r} 7 \\ + \Box \\ \hline 11 \end{array}
\quad
\begin{array}{r} 4 \\ + 7 \\ \hline \end{array}
\quad
\begin{array}{r} 11 \\ - \Box \\ \hline 4 \end{array}
\quad
\begin{array}{r} \Box \\ - 4 \\ \hline 7 \end{array}
$$

More Fact Families

All of the number sentences in a **fact family** use the same numbers.

8, 7, 15

$$\underline{8} + \underline{7} = \underline{15}$$
$$\underline{7} + \underline{8} = \underline{15}$$
$$\underline{15} - \underline{7} = \underline{8}$$
$$\underline{15} - \underline{8} = \underline{7}$$

Complete the **fact family**.

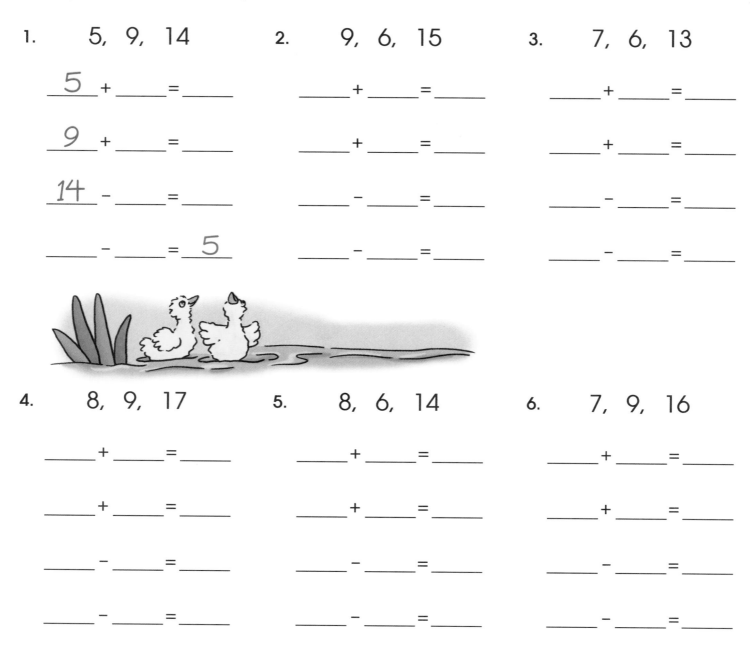

1. 5, 9, 14

$$\underline{5} + \underline{\quad} = \underline{\quad}$$
$$\underline{9} + \underline{\quad} = \underline{\quad}$$
$$\underline{14} - \underline{\quad} = \underline{\quad}$$
$$\underline{\quad} - \underline{\quad} = \underline{5}$$

2. 9, 6, 15

$$\underline{\quad} + \underline{\quad} = \underline{\quad}$$
$$\underline{\quad} + \underline{\quad} = \underline{\quad}$$
$$\underline{\quad} - \underline{\quad} = \underline{\quad}$$
$$\underline{\quad} - \underline{\quad} = \underline{\quad}$$

3. 7, 6, 13

$$\underline{\quad} + \underline{\quad} = \underline{\quad}$$
$$\underline{\quad} + \underline{\quad} = \underline{\quad}$$
$$\underline{\quad} - \underline{\quad} = \underline{\quad}$$
$$\underline{\quad} - \underline{\quad} = \underline{\quad}$$

4. 8, 9, 17

$$\underline{\quad} + \underline{\quad} = \underline{\quad}$$
$$\underline{\quad} + \underline{\quad} = \underline{\quad}$$
$$\underline{\quad} - \underline{\quad} = \underline{\quad}$$
$$\underline{\quad} - \underline{\quad} = \underline{\quad}$$

5. 8, 6, 14

$$\underline{\quad} + \underline{\quad} = \underline{\quad}$$
$$\underline{\quad} + \underline{\quad} = \underline{\quad}$$
$$\underline{\quad} - \underline{\quad} = \underline{\quad}$$
$$\underline{\quad} - \underline{\quad} = \underline{\quad}$$

6. 7, 9, 16

$$\underline{\quad} + \underline{\quad} = \underline{\quad}$$
$$\underline{\quad} + \underline{\quad} = \underline{\quad}$$
$$\underline{\quad} - \underline{\quad} = \underline{\quad}$$
$$\underline{\quad} - \underline{\quad} = \underline{\quad}$$

Which Number Is Missing?

Find the missing number. Use the number line if you need help.

0 1 2 3 4 5 6 7 8 9 10 11 12

1. 11
  - 2

2. 7
  - 4

3. 12
  - ☐
    8

4. 11
  - 7

5. 9
  - 5

6. ☐
  - 2
    5

7. 12
  - 7

8. 10
  - 3

9. 10
  - 8

10. 11
   - 3

11. 11
   - 8

12. 9
   - 3

13. 8
   - ☐
     5

14. 7
   - ☐
     4

15. ☐
   - 6
     4

16. ☐
   - 5
     5

Subtraction facts related to sums through 12

Which Numbers Are Missing?

Find the missing numbers.

1.
$$6 + \square = 10 \qquad 10 - \square = 4$$

2.
$$14 - 8 = \square \qquad 6 + \square = 14$$

3.
$$3 + \square = 12 \qquad 12 - \square = 9$$

4.
$$7 + \square = 13 \qquad 13 - \square = 6$$

5.
$$15 - 8 = \square \qquad \square + 7 = 15$$

6.
$$9 + \square = 18 \qquad \square - 9 = 9$$

7. $\square + 7 = 11$

$11 - 4 = \square$

8. $7 + \square = 14$

$\square - 7 = 7$

9. $6 + \square = 15$

$15 - 9 = \square$

10. $6 + \square = 12$

$\square - 6 = 6$

11. $8 + \square = 17$

$17 - \square = 9$

12. $13 - 8 = \square$

$5 + \square = 13$

Addition and subtraction facts; sums through 18

Solve the Riddle

Solve this riddle:
Which animal would you like to hire to work in an office?
Add or subtract to find the answer.

A
6 + 7 = _____

E
3 + 9 = _____

T
14 – 7 = _____

S
16 – 8 = _____

A
5 + 8 = _____

R
18 – 9 = _____

E
4 + 8 = _____

R
17 – 8 = _____

R
15 – 6 = _____

S
15 – 7 = _____

Y
8 + 6 = _____

C
9 + 6 = _____

D
7 + 9 = _____

B
9 + 8 = _____

I
14 – 9 = _____

The ___ ___ ___ ___ ___ ___ ___ ___ ___
     8   12 15 9   12 7   13 9   14

___ ___ ___ ___
17 5   9   16

Check the Facts

Put an **X** on the seven incorrect answers.
Write the correct answers.
Which set has **more** correct answers? _____

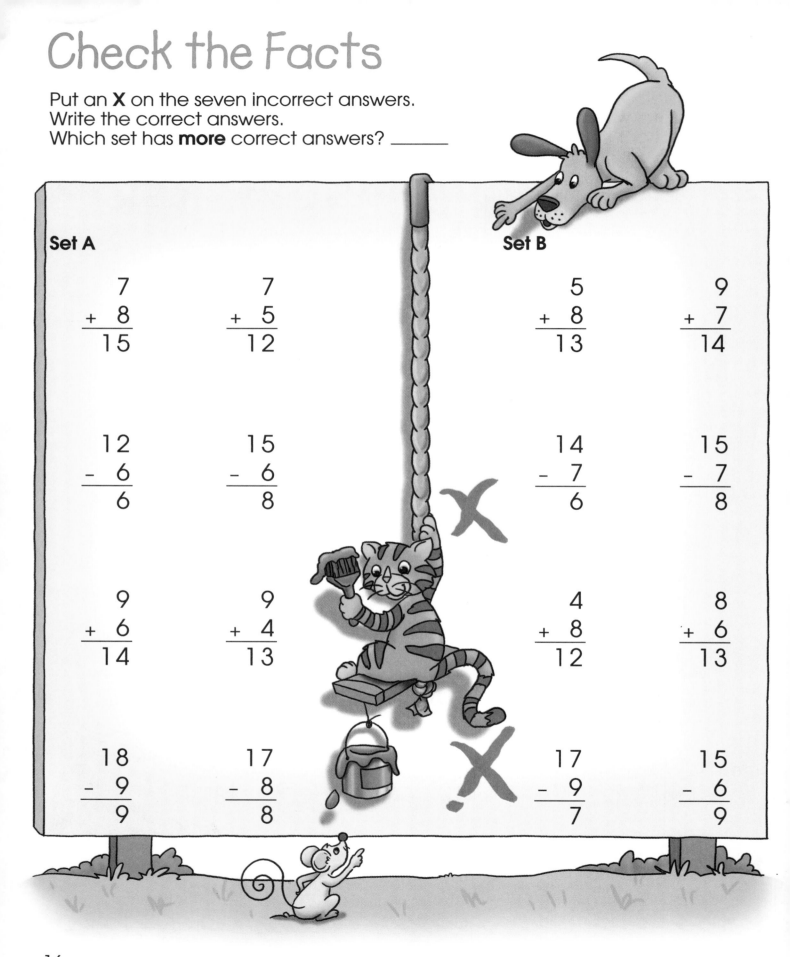

Set A

$$\begin{array}{r} 7 \\ +\ 8 \\ \hline 15 \end{array} \qquad \begin{array}{r} 7 \\ +\ 5 \\ \hline 12 \end{array}$$

$$\begin{array}{r} 12 \\ -\ 6 \\ \hline 6 \end{array} \qquad \begin{array}{r} 15 \\ -\ 6 \\ \hline 8 \end{array}$$

$$\begin{array}{r} 9 \\ +\ 6 \\ \hline 14 \end{array} \qquad \begin{array}{r} 9 \\ +\ 4 \\ \hline 13 \end{array}$$

$$\begin{array}{r} 18 \\ -\ 9 \\ \hline 9 \end{array} \qquad \begin{array}{r} 17 \\ -\ 8 \\ \hline 8 \end{array}$$

Set B

$$\begin{array}{r} 5 \\ +\ 8 \\ \hline 13 \end{array} \qquad \begin{array}{r} 9 \\ +\ 7 \\ \hline 14 \end{array}$$

$$\begin{array}{r} 14 \\ -\ 7 \\ \hline 6 \end{array} \qquad \begin{array}{r} 15 \\ -\ 7 \\ \hline 8 \end{array}$$

$$\begin{array}{r} 4 \\ +\ 8 \\ \hline 12 \end{array} \qquad \begin{array}{r} 8 \\ +\ 6 \\ \hline 13 \end{array}$$

$$\begin{array}{r} 17 \\ -\ 9 \\ \hline 7 \end{array} \qquad \begin{array}{r} 15 \\ -\ 6 \\ \hline 9 \end{array}$$

Addition and subtraction facts; sums through 18

Add More Numbers

$$\begin{array}{r} 7 \\ 6 \\ +\ 3 \\ \hline 16 \end{array}$$

You can add numbers in any order.
Look for tens to make the adding easier.
$$7 + 3 = 10$$
Then $10 + 6 = 16$.
It's easy!

It's a snap!

Find the **sum**.

1. $$\begin{array}{r} 4 \\ 3 \\ +\ 6 \\ \hline \end{array}$$

2. $$\begin{array}{r} 2 \\ 7 \\ +\ 8 \\ \hline \end{array}$$

3. $$\begin{array}{r} 5 \\ 6 \\ +\ 5 \\ \hline \end{array}$$

4. $$\begin{array}{r} 9 \\ 4 \\ +\ 1 \\ \hline \end{array}$$

5. $$\begin{array}{r} 3 \\ 8 \\ +\ 0 \\ \hline \end{array}$$

6. $$\begin{array}{r} 6 \\ 8 \\ +\ 4 \\ \hline \end{array}$$

7. $$\begin{array}{r} 2 \\ 3 \\ +\ 9 \\ \hline \end{array}$$

8. $$\begin{array}{r} 7 \\ 1 \\ +\ 7 \\ \hline \end{array}$$

9. $$\begin{array}{r} 6 \\ 2 \\ 5 \\ +\ 4 \\ \hline \end{array}$$

10. $$\begin{array}{r} 7 \\ 2 \\ 0 \\ +\ 3 \\ \hline \end{array}$$

11. $$\begin{array}{r} 3 \\ 4 \\ 5 \\ +\ 6 \\ \hline \end{array}$$

12. $$\begin{array}{r} 4 \\ 4 \\ 4 \\ +\ 4 \\ \hline \end{array}$$

13. $6 + 7 + 4 = \underline{\qquad}$

14. $7 + 2 + 3 = \underline{\qquad}$

15. $8 + 5 + 2 = \underline{\qquad}$

16. $9 + 0 + 9 = \underline{\qquad}$

17. $6 + 7 + 2 + 3 = \underline{\qquad}$

18. $4 + 5 + 6 + 5 = \underline{\qquad}$

Same Sums Across and Down

Each row and column has the same sum.
Fill in the **sums** and missing **addends**.

1.   **Sums of 10**

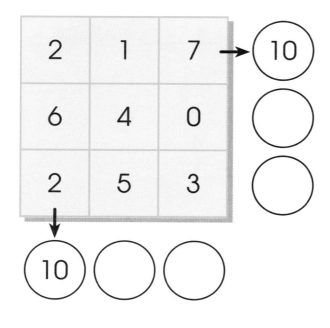

2.   **Sums of 15**

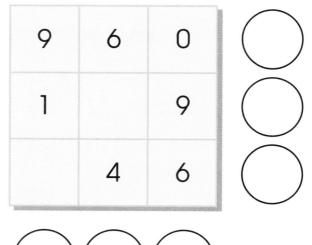

3.   **Sums of 16**

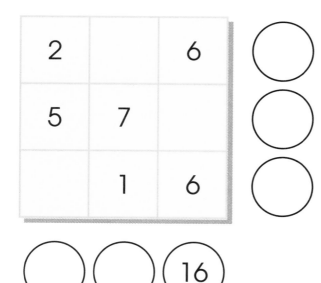

4.   **Sums of 18**

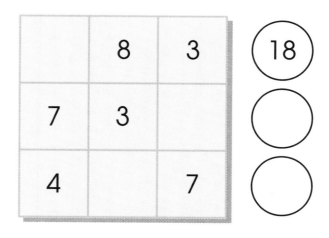

Add or Subtract

Find each **sum** or **difference**.

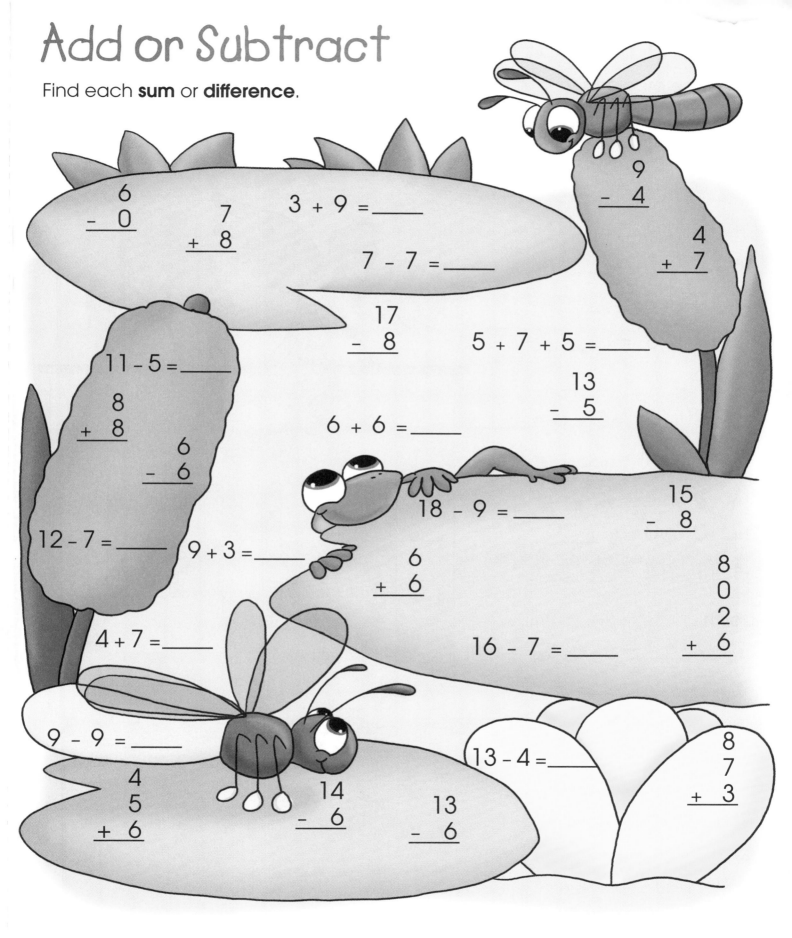

$$\begin{array}{r} 6 \\ -\ 0 \\ \hline \end{array}$$

$$\begin{array}{r} 7 \\ +\ 8 \\ \hline \end{array}$$

$3 + 9 =$ _____

$7 - 7 =$ _____

$$\begin{array}{r} 9 \\ -\ 4 \\ \hline \end{array}$$

$$\begin{array}{r} 4 \\ +\ 7 \\ \hline \end{array}$$

$$\begin{array}{r} 17 \\ -\ 8 \\ \hline \end{array}$$

$5 + 7 + 5 =$ _____

$11 - 5 =$ _____

$$\begin{array}{r} 8 \\ +\ 8 \\ \hline \end{array}$$

$$\begin{array}{r} 6 \\ -\ 6 \\ \hline \end{array}$$

$$\begin{array}{r} 13 \\ -\ 5 \\ \hline \end{array}$$

$6 + 6 =$ _____

$12 - 7 =$ _____

$9 + 3 =$ _____

$18 - 9 =$ _____

$$\begin{array}{r} 15 \\ -\ 8 \\ \hline \end{array}$$

$$\begin{array}{r} 6 \\ +\ 6 \\ \hline \end{array}$$

$4 + 7 =$ _____

$16 - 7 =$ _____

$$\begin{array}{r} 8 \\ 0 \\ 2 \\ +\ 6 \\ \hline \end{array}$$

$9 - 9 =$ _____

$13 - 4 =$ _____

$$\begin{array}{r} 4 \\ 5 \\ +\ 6 \\ \hline \end{array}$$

$$\begin{array}{r} 14 \\ -\ 6 \\ \hline \end{array}$$

$$\begin{array}{r} 13 \\ -\ 6 \\ \hline \end{array}$$

$$\begin{array}{r} 8 \\ 7 \\ +\ 3 \\ \hline \end{array}$$

Addition and Subtraction Puzzle

Solve the problems to fill in the puzzle.

Across

1. $3 + 8 =$ _11_
3. $6 + 0 =$ _____
4. $5 + 6 =$ _____
5. $7 + 7 =$ _____
7. $16 - 7 =$ _____
9. $14 - 8 =$ _____
10. $9 + 9 =$ _____
11. $2 + 3 + 4 + 5 =$ _____
12. $8 + 8 =$ _____
13. $5 + 5 + 2 + 5 =$ _____
14. $10 - 0 =$ _____
15. $11 - 4 =$ _____

Down

2. $7 + 9 =$ _____
4. $5 + 9 =$ _____
5. $6 + 4 + 3 =$ _____
6. $4 + 3 + 9 =$ _____
8. $3 + 8 + 7 =$ _____
10. $8 + 8 =$ _____
11. $9 + 8 =$ _____
12. $4 + 6 =$ _____

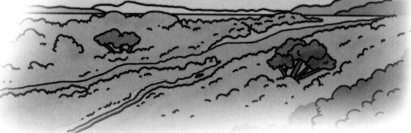

Addition and subtraction facts; sums through 18   © School Zone Publishing Company

Problem Solving

4 dogs are sleeping.
6 dogs are playing.
How many dogs are there altogether?

Read: What is the problem asking?

Plan: (add) or subtract

Solve: **4 + 6 = 10**

Check: How many dogs are there altogether? There are 10 dogs.

Write the number sentence for the problem.

1. There are 5 goldfish.
   There are 6 striped fish.
   How many fish are there in all?

   _____ __ _____ = _____

2. There were 11 flowers in a garden.
   7 flowers were picked.
   How many flowers were left?

   _____ __ _____ = _____

3. There are 7 bluebirds in a tree.
   3 blackbirds join them.
   How many birds are there altogether?

   _____ __ _____ = _____

4. There are 13 purple flowers.
   There are 9 pink flowers.
   How many more purple flowers are there?

   _____ __ _____ = _____

More Problem Solving

Remember:
Read
Plan
Solve
Check

Write the number sentence for the problem.

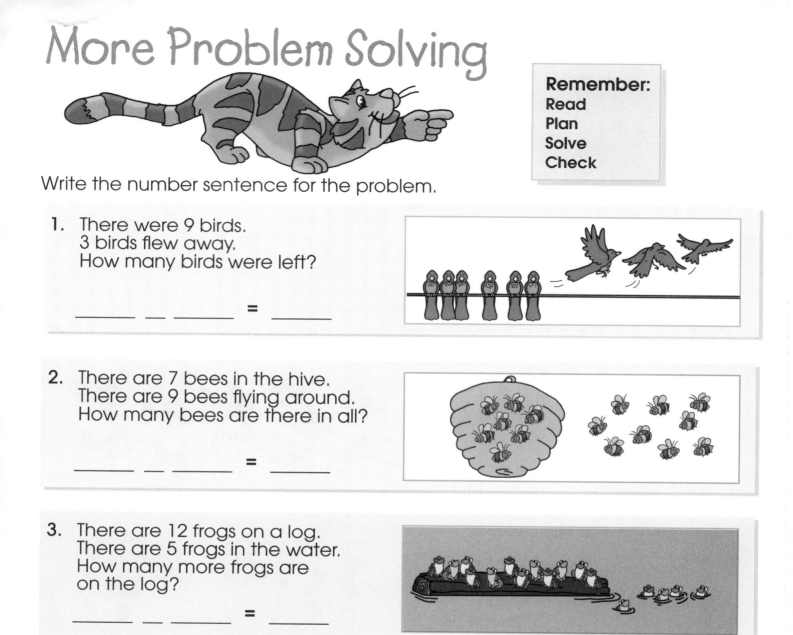

1. There were 9 birds.
   3 birds flew away.
   How many birds were left?

   _____ __ _____ = _____

2. There are 7 bees in the hive.
   There are 9 bees flying around.
   How many bees are there in all?

   _____ __ _____ = _____

3. There are 12 frogs on a log.
   There are 5 frogs in the water.
   How many more frogs are
   on the log?

   _____ __ _____ = _____

4. 17 cats are sleeping.
   5 cats are playing.
   How many cats are there
   altogether?

   _____ __ _____ = _____

5. There are 6 mums.
   There are 8 roses.
   How many flowers are there in all?

   _____ __ _____ = _____

Tens and Ones

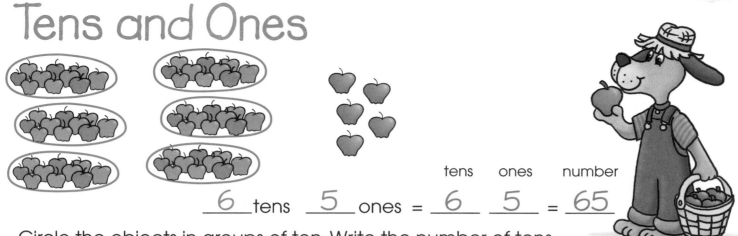

tens   ones   number

__6__ tens __5__ ones = __6__ __5__ = __65__

Circle the objects in groups of ten. Write the number of tens and ones. Then write the number.

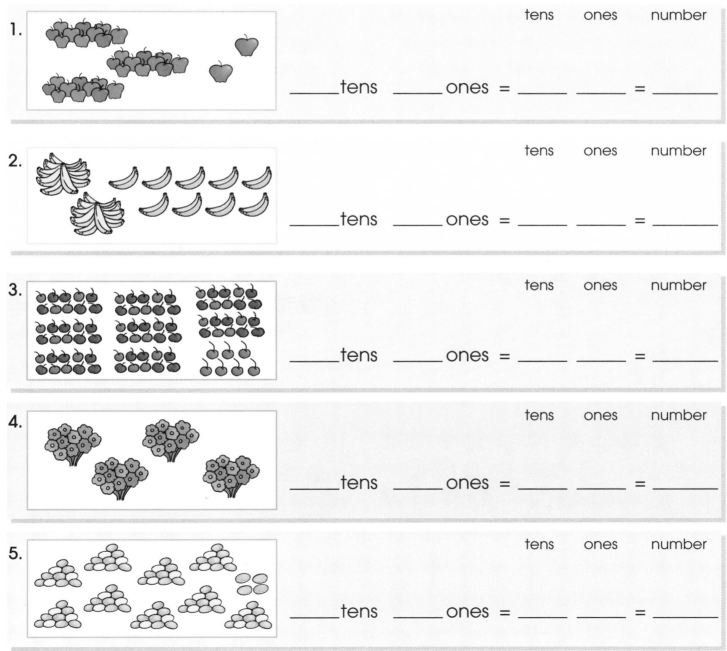

1.
tens   ones   number

_____tens _____ ones = _____ _____ = _____

2.
tens   ones   number

_____tens _____ ones = _____ _____ = _____

3.
tens   ones   number

_____tens _____ ones = _____ _____ = _____

4.
tens   ones   number

_____tens _____ ones = _____ _____ = _____

5.
tens   ones   number

_____tens _____ ones = _____ _____ = _____

More about Tens and Ones

___2___ tens ___6___ ones

How many? ___26___

Circle the objects in groups of ten. Write the number of tens and ones.
Then write how many there are in all.

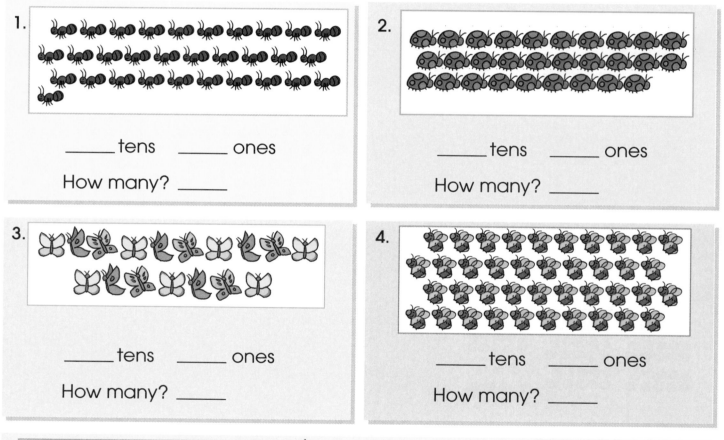

1.

_____ tens _____ ones

How many? _____

2.

_____ tens _____ ones

How many? _____

3.

_____ tens _____ ones

How many? _____

4.

_____ tens _____ ones

How many? _____

5.

_____ tens _____ ones

How many? _____

Match Tens and Ones

Match each group to the correct number.

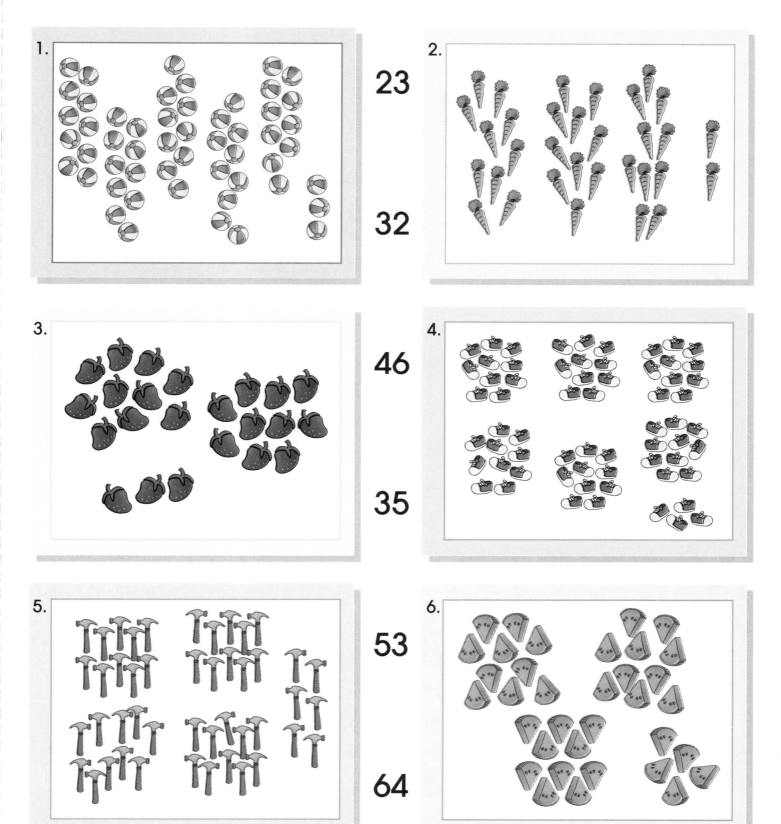

1.

23

32

2.

3.

46

35

4.

5.

53

64

6.

How Many?

Count the number of objects. Then write the number.

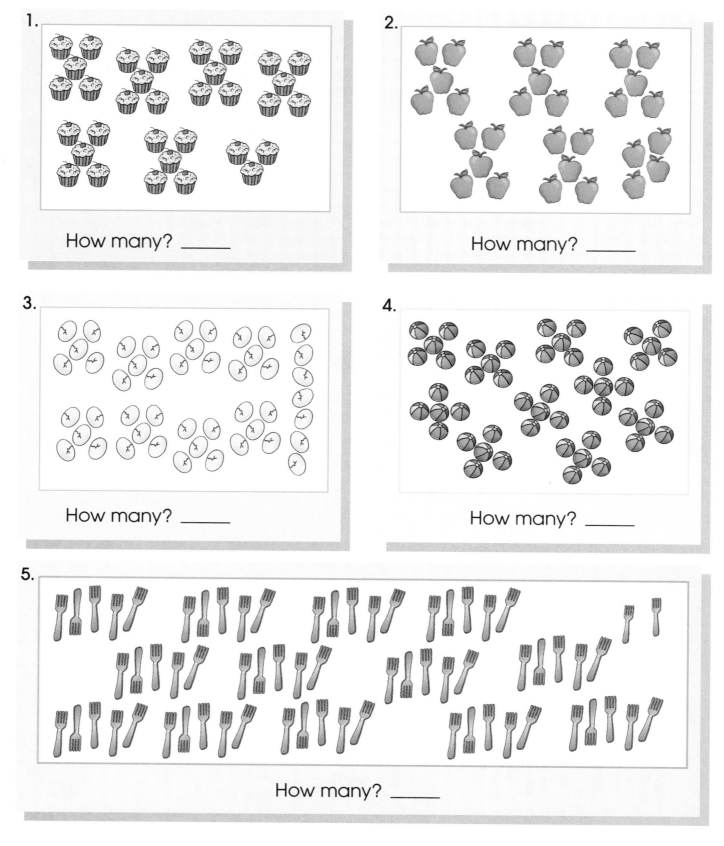

1.

How many? _____

2.

How many? _____

3.

How many? _____

4.

How many? _____

5.

How many? _____

Understanding two-digit numbers

Numbers and Number Names

1 one	11 eleven
2 two	12 twelve
3 three	13 thirteen
4 four	14 fourteen
5 five	15 fifteen
6 six	16 sixteen
7 seven	17 seventeen
8 eight	18 eighteen
9 nine	19 nineteen
10 ten	

_1_ ten _4_ ones

Number: _14_

Number name: **fourteen**

Write the number.

1. seven _____   2. ten _____   3. eight _____

4. fifteen _____   5. eleven _____   6. eighteen _____

Write the number or number name.

7. 13 ones _____   8. 1 ten 4 ones _____

9. 1 ten 9 ones _____   10. 12 _____

11. 16 _____   12. 17 _____

More Number Names

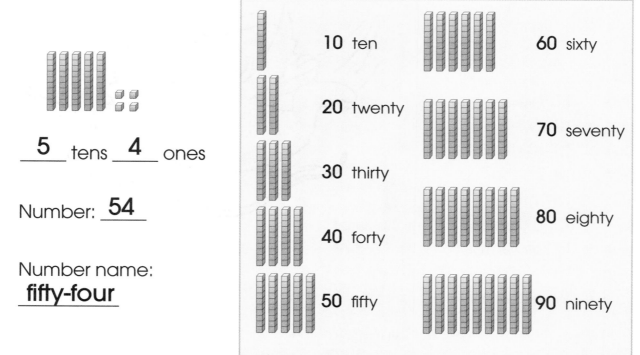

_____5_____ tens _____4_____ ones

Number: ___54___

Number name:
fifty-four

10 ten

20 twenty

30 thirty

40 forty

50 fifty

60 sixty

70 seventy

80 eighty

90 ninety

Write how many tens and ones there are. Then write the number and number name.

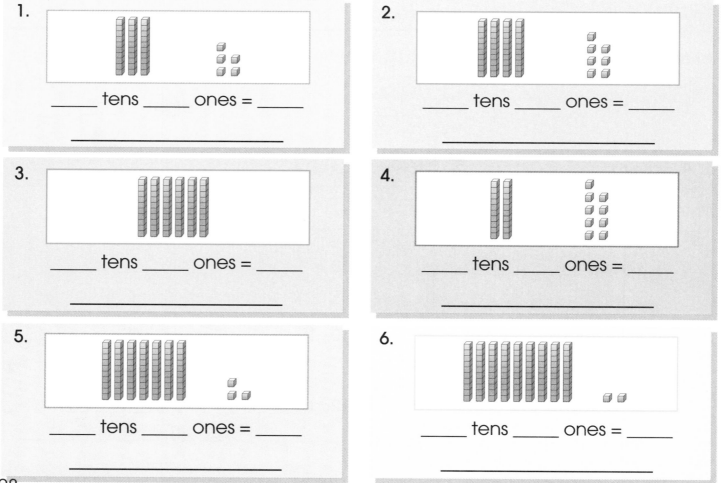

1. _____ tens _____ ones = _____

   _____

2. _____ tens _____ ones = _____

   _____

3. _____ tens _____ ones = _____

   _____

4. _____ tens _____ ones = _____

   _____

5. _____ tens _____ ones = _____

   _____

6. _____ tens _____ ones = _____

   _____

Count to 100

Complete the chart. Count to 100.

1	2	3		5			8		10
11		13			16			19	
21						27			30
	32		34				38		
		43			46				50
51				55				59	
			64			67			70
	72				76		78		
81		83						89	
		94					98		100

Count by tens.
Circle the tens.

tens

Count by fives.
Circle the fives.

fives

Count by Twos, Fives, and Tens

Connect the dots.
Start at the ▲ and count by 2s to 50.
Start at the ● and count by 5s to 100.
Start at the ■ and count by 10s to 100.

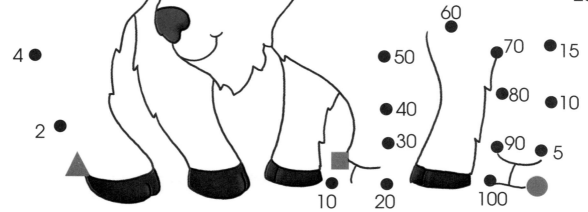

Which Numbers Are Missing?

Write the missing numbers.

1. 21, 22, _____, 24, _____, 26, _____, 28, _____, 30

2. 61, _____, 63, _____, _____, 66, _____, _____, 69, _____

3. _____, 82, _____, 84, _____, 86, _____, 88, _____, 90

4. 35, 36, _____, 38, _____, 40, _____, _____, 43, _____

5. 56, _____, 58, 59, _____, 61, _____, _____, 64, _____

6. 87, _____, 89, _____, _____, 92, _____, _____, 95, _____

7. 44, 43, _____, 41, _____, 39, _____, _____, 36, _____

8. _____, 73, _____, 71, _____, _____, 68, _____, _____, 65

Skip Counting

10, 12, 14, _16_, _18_, _20_

Find the pattern. Write the missing numbers.

1. 10, 20, _____, 40, _____, 60, 70, _____

2. 5, 10, _____, 20, 25, _____, 35, _____

3. 10, _____, 14, 16, _____, _____, 22, _____

4. 30, _____, 50, _____, _____, 80, _____, 100

5. 25, _____, 35, _____, _____, 50, 55, _____

6. 20, _____, _____, 26, 28, _____, _____, 34

Before and After

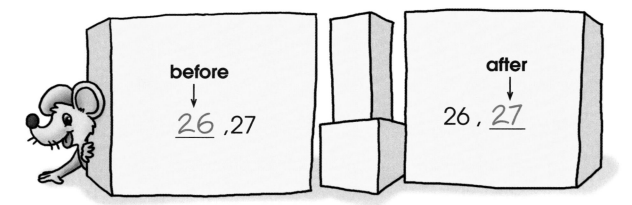

before
↓
<u>26</u> ,27

after
↓
26 , <u>27</u>

Which number comes **before**?

1. _____ ,53   2. _____ ,20   3. _____ ,45

4. _____ ,37   5. _____ ,88   6. _____ ,71

7. _____ ,100   8. _____ ,60   9. _____ ,79

Which number comes **after**?

10. 34, _____   11. 46, _____   12. 51, _____

13. 49, _____   14. 25, _____   15. 73, _____

16. 60, _____   17. 82, _____   18. 79, _____

Before, Between, and After

before
↓
<u>23</u> , 24 , 25

23, <u>24</u> , 25
↑
between

after
↓
23, 24, <u>25</u>

Which number comes **before**?

1. _____ , 34, 35

2. _____ , 40, 41

3. _____ , 94, 95

4. _____ , 71, 72

5. _____ , 28, 29

6. _____ , 52, 53

Which number belongs **between**?

7. 27, _____ , 29

8. 61, _____ , 63

9. 76, _____ , 78

10. 40, _____ , 42

11. 47, _____ , 49

12. 69, _____ , 71

Which number comes **after**?

13. 45, 46, _____

14. 81, 82, _____

15. 28, 29, _____

16. 66, 67, _____

17. 98, 99, _____

18. 37, 38, _____

Concepts of *before, between,* and *after*

Before, Between, and After

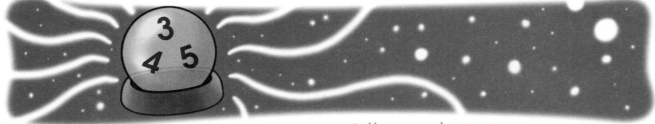

<u>34 and 35</u> come **before** 39.

Find and write all the two-digit numbers that make the sentence true.

1.

_____ come **after** 46.

2.

_____ come **before** 60.

3.

_____ come **before** 85.

4.

_____ come **after** 57.

5.

_____ come **between** 50 and 60.

6.

_____ come **between** 47 and 70.

Concepts of before, between, and after

Greater or Less

Look at the tens digits in both numbers first and compare.
If the tens digits are the same, look at the ones digits.

3 tens 4 ones

34
↑
less

4 tens 3 ones

43
↑
greater

This number has more tens.

Circle the number that is **greater**.

1. 65   68   2. 74   84   3. 39   93

4. 70   17   5. 25   62   6. 88   78

7. 40   39   8. 90   9   9. 55   62

Circle the number that is **less**.

10. 77   79   11. 18   80   12. 20   32

13. 65   71   14. 43   48   15. 70   63

16. 91   99   17. 77   69   18. 82   28

Greater Than or Less Than

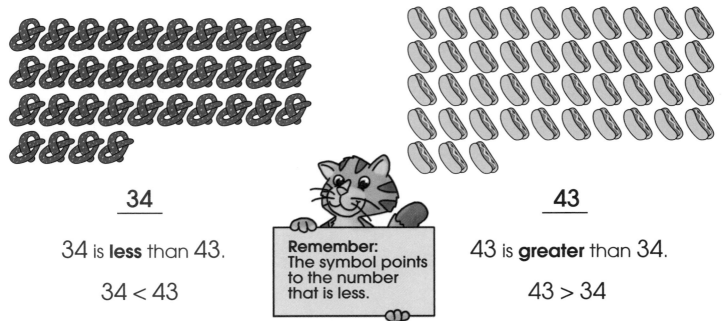

__34__

34 is **less** than 43.

34 < 43

Remember: The symbol points to the number that is less.

__43__

43 is **greater** than 34.

43 > 34

Write the numbers for each group. Circle < or > between the numbers.

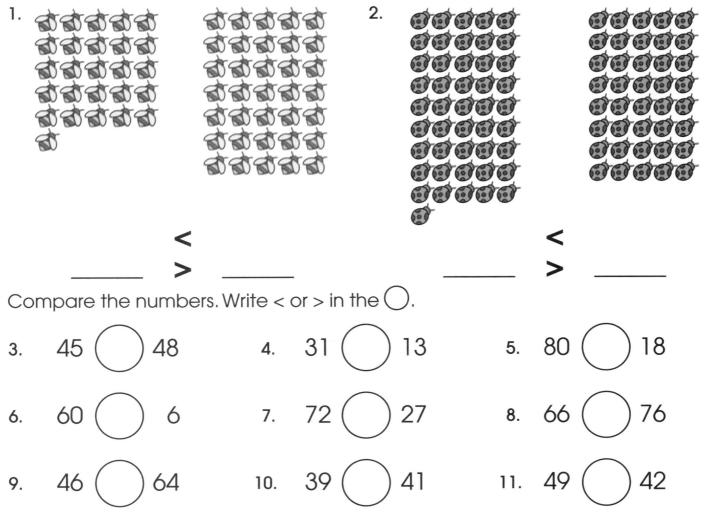

1. _____ < / > _____

2. _____ < / > _____

Compare the numbers. Write < or > in the ◯.

3. 45 ◯ 48

4. 31 ◯ 13

5. 80 ◯ 18

6. 60 ◯ 6

7. 72 ◯ 27

8. 66 ◯ 76

9. 46 ◯ 64

10. 39 ◯ 41

11. 49 ◯ 42

Concepts of *greater than* and *less than*   37

Number Order

Write the numbers in order from **least** to **greatest**.

1. 12   10   15

2. 45   49   36

_____ _____ _____

3. 81   19   25

4. 36   24   18

_____ _____ _____

5. 29   57   41

6. 30   72   55

_____ _____ _____

7. 66   26   56

8. 87   78   72

_____ _____ _____

Tens and Ones

__2__ tens __3__ ones = __23__

Write the number of tens and ones. Then write the number.

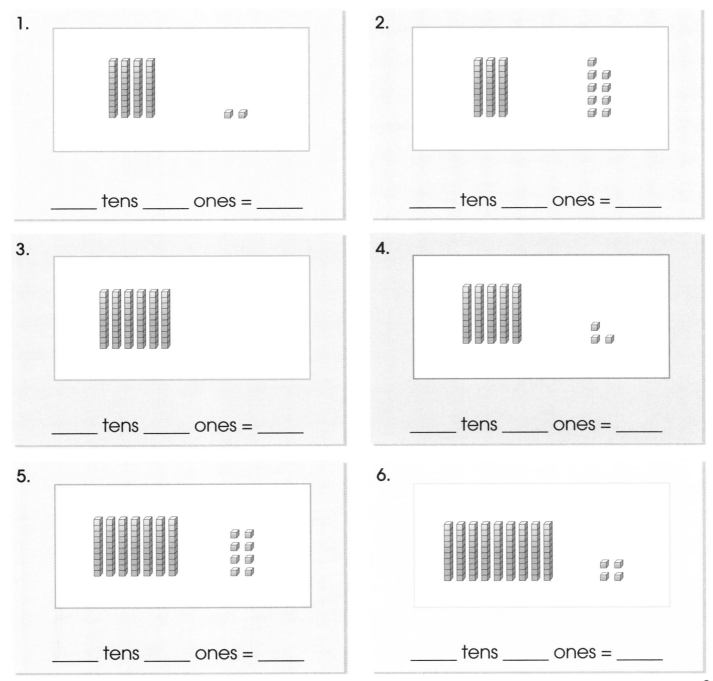

1.

_____ tens _____ ones = _____

2.

_____ tens _____ ones = _____

3.

_____ tens _____ ones = _____

4.

_____ tens _____ ones = _____

5.

_____ tens _____ ones = _____

6.

_____ tens _____ ones = _____

Match Tens and Ones

Match each group to the correct number.

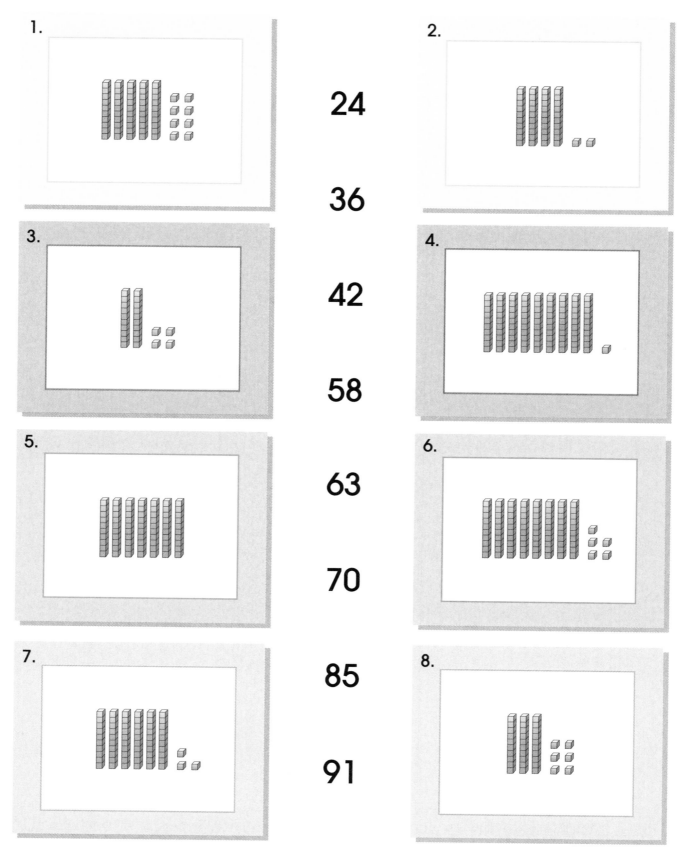

1.

2.

24

36

3.

4.

42

58

5.

63

6.

70

7.

85

91

8.

Compare Numbers

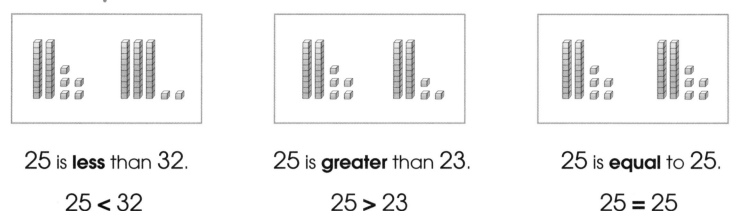

25 is **less** than 32.

25 < 32

25 is **greater** than 23.

25 > 23

25 is **equal** to 25.

25 = 25

Write the numbers. Compare the numbers. Then write <, >, or = in the ◯.

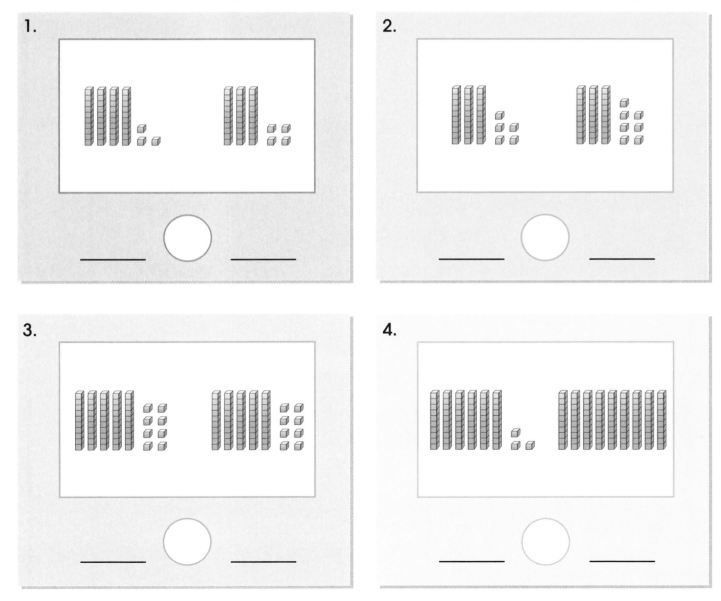

1.

_____ ◯ _____

2.

_____ ◯ _____

3.

_____ ◯ _____

4.

_____ ◯ _____

Compare More Numbers

26 < 36
↑
more tens

45 > 4 tens
45 > 40
↑
more ones

twelve < 21
12 < 21
↑
more tens

Remember:
The symbol points
to the number
that is less.

Compare the numbers. Then write <, >, or = in the ◯.

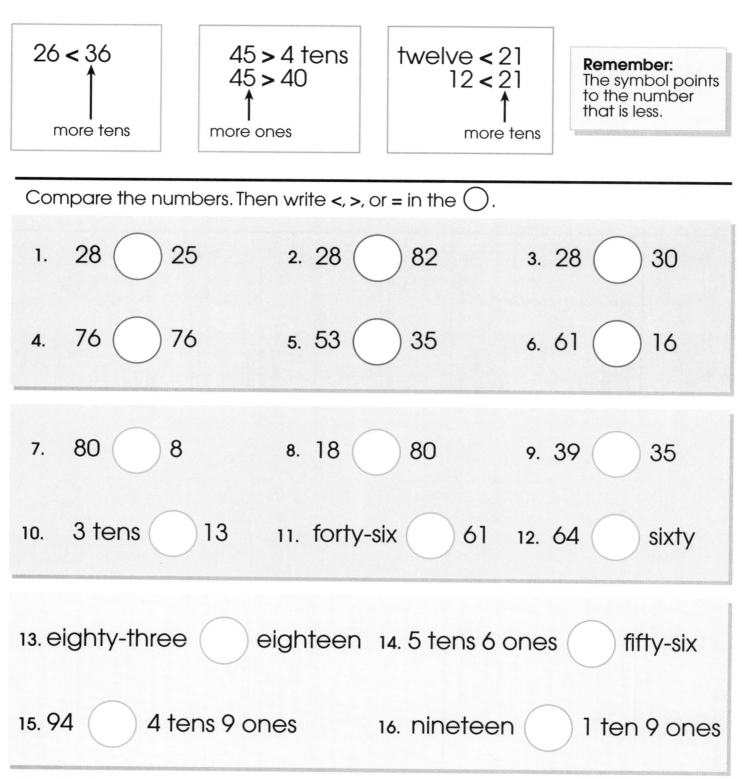

1. 28 ◯ 25

2. 28 ◯ 82

3. 28 ◯ 30

4. 76 ◯ 76

5. 53 ◯ 35

6. 61 ◯ 16

7. 80 ◯ 8

8. 18 ◯ 80

9. 39 ◯ 35

10. 3 tens ◯ 13

11. forty-six ◯ 61

12. 64 ◯ sixty

13. eighty-three ◯ eighteen

14. 5 tens 6 ones ◯ fifty-six

15. 94 ◯ 4 tens 9 ones

16. nineteen ◯ 1 ten 9 ones

17. **Challenge:** I am less than 50. I am greater than 39. My tens digit is 2 more than my ones digit. What number am I? _____

Even and Odd Numbers

An **even number** of things can be matched in pairs.

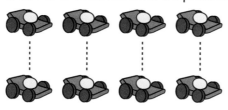

8 is an **even** number.

An **odd number** of things cannot be matched in pairs.

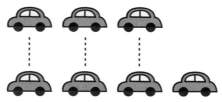

7 is an **odd** number.

Match up the objects in pairs if you can. Count the objects and write the number. Tell whether the number is **even** or **odd**.

1.

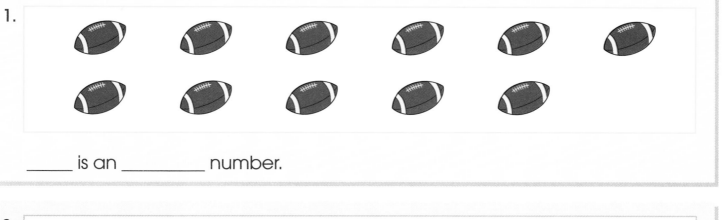

_____ is an _____ number.

2.

_____ is an _____ number.

3.

_____ is an _____ number.

Even or Odd?

1. Count by 2s and circle the numbers.

2. You circled even numbers. Look at the ones digit of the circled numbers. The ones digit of an **even** number is:

1	2	3	4	5	6	7	8	9	10
11	12	13	14	15	16	17	18	19	20
21	22	23	24	25	26	27	28	29	30
31	32	33	34	35	36	37	38	39	40

   _____, _____, _____, _____, or _____.

3. The numbers in the chart that are not circled are odd numbers. The ones digit of an **odd** number is:

   _____, _____, _____, _____, or _____.

Write **even** or **odd**.

4. 27_____

5. 38_____

6. 50_____

7. 62_____

8. 45_____

9. 79_____

10. Circle the **even** numbers.   23   6   47   18   64   80   35   58   96

Sum It Up
Write **even** or **odd**. Show an example for each problem.

11. The sum of two even numbers is an _____ number.

    Example: _____

12. The sum of two odd numbers is an _____ number.

    Example: _____

13. The sum of an even number and an odd number is an _____ number.

    Example: _____

Ordinal Numbers

An **ordinal number** tells the position of an object.

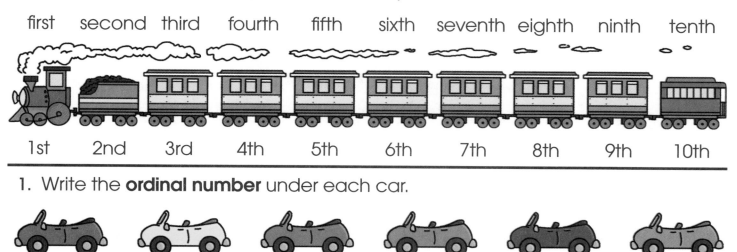

| first | second | third | fourth | fifth | sixth | seventh | eighth | ninth | tenth |
| 1st | 2nd | 3rd | 4th | 5th | 6th | 7th | 8th | 9th | 10th |

1. Write the **ordinal number** under each car.

1st _____ 3rd _____ _____ _____

2. Write the **ordinal number word** under each car.

seventh _____ _____ tenth

Write the ordinal number, child's name, or number in each blank.

3. If Andy is first, then Chris is _____. If Ben is second, then Emma is _____.

4. If David is fourth, how many people are ahead of him? _____

5. If Andy is first, then _____ is the 7th person in line.

6. **Challenge:** If Ken is first, then who is 6th in line? _____

Ordinal Number Riddles

Use the **ordinal number** clues to solve each riddle.

1. It's a big smile.

READING

- 7th letter
- 1st letter
- 5th letter
- 6th letter

G ☐ ☐ ☐

2. You use clocks to tell it.

ARITHMETIC

- 4th letter
- 3rd letter
- 6th letter
- 7th letter

☐ ☐ ☐ ☐

3. You walk on it.

ORDINAL

- 7th letter
- 6th letter
- 5th letter
- 3rd letter

☐ ☐ ☐ ☐

4. They are purr-fect animals.

SUBTRACT

- 7th letter
- 6th letter
- 4th letter
- 1st letter

☐ ☐ ☐ ☐

46　Ordinal numbers: 1st through 10th

Add Ones to Numbers

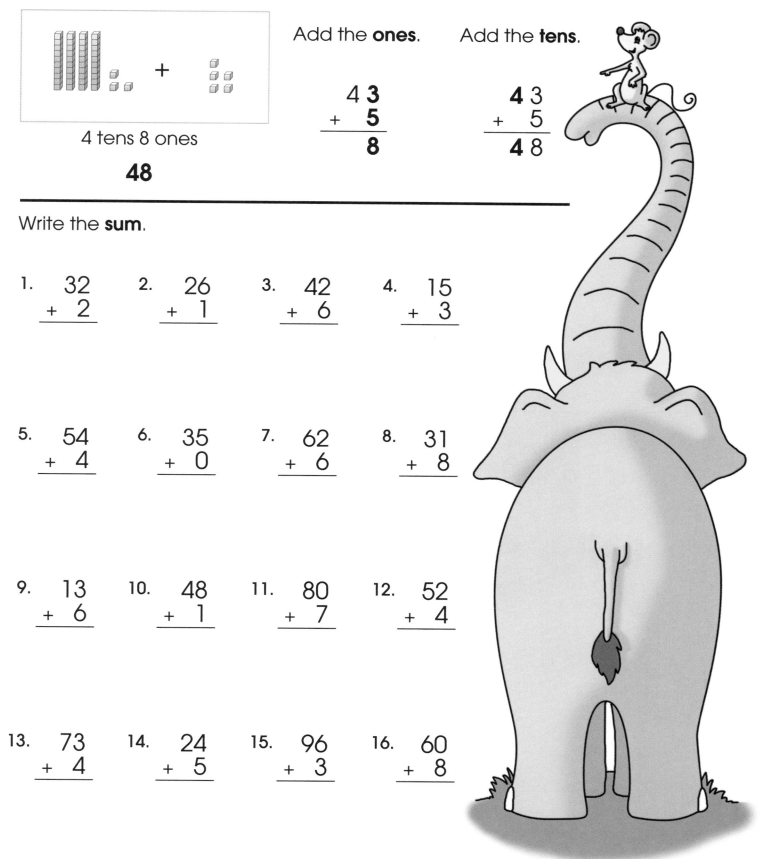

4 tens 8 ones

48

Add the **ones**.

$$\begin{array}{r} 4\mathbf{3} \\ +\ \ \mathbf{5} \\ \hline \mathbf{8} \end{array}$$

Add the **tens**.

$$\begin{array}{r} \mathbf{4}3 \\ +\ \ 5 \\ \hline \mathbf{4}8 \end{array}$$

Write the **sum**.

1. $\begin{array}{r} 32 \\ +\ 2 \\ \hline \end{array}$

2. $\begin{array}{r} 26 \\ +\ 1 \\ \hline \end{array}$

3. $\begin{array}{r} 42 \\ +\ 6 \\ \hline \end{array}$

4. $\begin{array}{r} 15 \\ +\ 3 \\ \hline \end{array}$

5. $\begin{array}{r} 54 \\ +\ 4 \\ \hline \end{array}$

6. $\begin{array}{r} 35 \\ +\ 0 \\ \hline \end{array}$

7. $\begin{array}{r} 62 \\ +\ 6 \\ \hline \end{array}$

8. $\begin{array}{r} 31 \\ +\ 8 \\ \hline \end{array}$

9. $\begin{array}{r} 13 \\ +\ 6 \\ \hline \end{array}$

10. $\begin{array}{r} 48 \\ +\ 1 \\ \hline \end{array}$

11. $\begin{array}{r} 80 \\ +\ 7 \\ \hline \end{array}$

12. $\begin{array}{r} 52 \\ +\ 4 \\ \hline \end{array}$

13. $\begin{array}{r} 73 \\ +\ 4 \\ \hline \end{array}$

14. $\begin{array}{r} 24 \\ +\ 5 \\ \hline \end{array}$

15. $\begin{array}{r} 96 \\ +\ 3 \\ \hline \end{array}$

16. $\begin{array}{r} 60 \\ +\ 8 \\ \hline \end{array}$

Add on Ones

Solve the problems to fill in the puzzle.

	1. **1**	2. **9**		3.	4.
5.		6.	7.		8.
10.	11.		12.	13.	
	14.	15.		16.	17.
18.		19.	20.		21.
23.	24.		25.	26.	

Across

1. $\begin{array}{r} 18 \\ +\ 1 \\ \hline 19 \end{array}$ 3. $\begin{array}{r} 44 \\ +\ 2 \\ \hline \end{array}$ 6. $\begin{array}{r} 38 \\ +\ 0 \\ \hline \end{array}$

8. $\begin{array}{r} 53 \\ +\ 4 \\ \hline \end{array}$ 10. $\begin{array}{r} 31 \\ +\ 8 \\ \hline \end{array}$ 12. $\begin{array}{r} 77 \\ +\ 2 \\ \hline \end{array}$

14. $\begin{array}{r} 45 \\ +\ 4 \\ \hline \end{array}$ 16. $\begin{array}{r} 25 \\ +\ 3 \\ \hline \end{array}$ 19. $\begin{array}{r} 20 \\ +\ 9 \\ \hline \end{array}$

21. $\begin{array}{r} 33 \\ +\ 3 \\ \hline \end{array}$ 23. $\begin{array}{r} 85 \\ +\ 3 \\ \hline \end{array}$ 25. $\begin{array}{r} 47 \\ +\ 2 \\ \hline \end{array}$

Down

2. $\begin{array}{r} 93 \\ +\ 0 \\ \hline \end{array}$ 4. $\begin{array}{r} 63 \\ +\ 2 \\ \hline \end{array}$ 5. $\begin{array}{r} 41 \\ +\ 2 \\ \hline \end{array}$ 7. $\begin{array}{r} 84 \\ +\ 3 \\ \hline \end{array}$ 9. $\begin{array}{r} 75 \\ +\ 4 \\ \hline \end{array}$ 11. $\begin{array}{r} 92 \\ +\ 2 \\ \hline \end{array}$

13. $\begin{array}{r} 90 \\ +\ 2 \\ \hline \end{array}$ 15. $\begin{array}{r} 91 \\ +\ 1 \\ \hline \end{array}$ 17. $\begin{array}{r} 82 \\ +\ 1 \\ \hline \end{array}$ 18. $\begin{array}{r} 55 \\ +\ 3 \\ \hline \end{array}$ 20. $\begin{array}{r} 90 \\ +\ 4 \\ \hline \end{array}$ 24. $\begin{array}{r} 86 \\ +\ 3 \\ \hline \end{array}$ 26. $\begin{array}{r} 95 \\ +\ 3 \\ \hline \end{array}$

Add Two-Digit Numbers

6 tens 9 ones
69

Add the **ones**.

```
  45
+ 24
───
   9
```

Add the **tens**.

```
  45
+ 24
───
  69
```

Find the **sum**.

1.
```
  32
+ 14
```

2.
```
  27
+ 42
```

3.
```
  51
+ 30
```

4.
```
  75
+ 12
```

5.
```
  33
+ 44
```

6.
```
  62
+ 24
```

7.
```
  47
+ 40
```

8.
```
  17
+ 31
```

9.
```
  83
+ 15
```

10.
```
  44
+ 25
```

11.
```
  68
+ 30
```

12.
```
  33
+ 33
```

13.
```
  26
+ 71
```

14.
```
  19
+ 80
```

15.
```
  70
+ 20
```

16.
```
  49
+ 50
```

Add Two-Digit Numbers

Find the **sum**.
Circle the **sums** with these colors:

yellow 35-58   red 59-75

orange 76-90   brown 91-99

Then color the spots on the giraffe.

Numbers on giraffe: 70, 58, 76, 97, 49, 75, 37, 89, 40, 55, 87, 98, 88, 59, 69, 98

1. $\begin{array}{r} 14 \\ + 23 \\ \hline \end{array}$ 2. $\begin{array}{r} 53 \\ + 22 \\ \hline \end{array}$ 3. $\begin{array}{r} 38 \\ + 11 \\ \hline \end{array}$ 4. $\begin{array}{r} 50 \\ + 20 \\ \hline \end{array}$

5. $\begin{array}{r} 45 \\ + 13 \\ \hline \end{array}$ 6. $\begin{array}{r} 62 \\ + 14 \\ \hline \end{array}$ 7. $\begin{array}{r} 77 \\ + 21 \\ \hline \end{array}$ 8. $\begin{array}{r} 45 \\ + 44 \\ \hline \end{array}$

9. $\begin{array}{r} 20 \\ + 20 \\ \hline \end{array}$ 10. $\begin{array}{r} 35 \\ + 52 \\ \hline \end{array}$ 11. $\begin{array}{r} 88 \\ + 10 \\ \hline \end{array}$ 12. $\begin{array}{r} 55 \\ + 14 \\ \hline \end{array}$

13. $\begin{array}{r} 56 \\ + 32 \\ \hline \end{array}$ 14. $\begin{array}{r} 14 \\ + 41 \\ \hline \end{array}$ 15. $\begin{array}{r} 12 \\ + 47 \\ \hline \end{array}$ 16. $\begin{array}{r} 23 \\ + 74 \\ \hline \end{array}$

Clue: There should be 5 yellow spots, 4 red spots, 4 orange spots, and 3 brown spots.

Add in Your Head

Add to finish the number wheels. Use mental math.

Adding one-digit and two-digit numbers without regrouping 51

Find Missing Addends

Write the missing number in the ☐.

1.
$$\begin{array}{r} 23 \\ + \boxed{4} \\ \hline 27 \end{array}$$

2.
$$\begin{array}{r} \boxed{} \\ + 20 \\ \hline 63 \end{array}$$

3.
$$\begin{array}{r} 50 \\ + \boxed{} \\ \hline 70 \end{array}$$

4.
$$\begin{array}{r} 31 \\ + \boxed{} \\ \hline 38 \end{array}$$

5.
$$\begin{array}{r} 46 \\ + \boxed{} \\ \hline 76 \end{array}$$

6.
$$\begin{array}{r} 41 \\ + \boxed{} \\ \hline 49 \end{array}$$

7.
$$\begin{array}{r} 79 \\ + \boxed{} \\ \hline 79 \end{array}$$

8.
$$\begin{array}{r} 79 \\ + \boxed{} \\ \hline 89 \end{array}$$

9.
$$\begin{array}{r} \boxed{} \\ + 8 \\ \hline 38 \end{array}$$

10.
$$\begin{array}{r} 62 \\ + \boxed{} \\ \hline 73 \end{array}$$

11.
$$\begin{array}{r} 35 \\ + \boxed{} \\ \hline 39 \end{array}$$

12.
$$\begin{array}{r} \boxed{} \\ + 5 \\ \hline 85 \end{array}$$

13.
$$\begin{array}{r} \boxed{} \\ + 9 \\ \hline 69 \end{array}$$

14.
$$\begin{array}{r} \boxed{} \\ + 14 \\ \hline 55 \end{array}$$

15.
$$\begin{array}{r} \boxed{} \\ + 7 \\ \hline 29 \end{array}$$

16.
$$\begin{array}{r} 30 \\ + \boxed{} \\ \hline 90 \end{array}$$

Adding one-digit and two-digit numbers without regrouping

Subtract Ones from Numbers

Subtract the **ones**.

```
  tens ones
    4 9
  -   5
  -----
      4
```

Subtract the **tens**.

```
  tens ones
    4 9
  -   5
  -----
    4 4
```

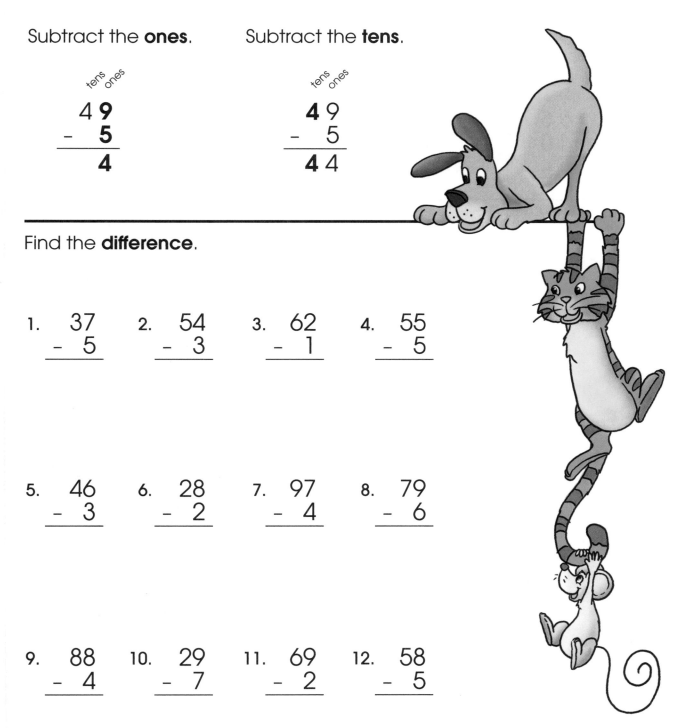

Find the **difference**.

1. 37
    - 5

2. 54
    - 3

3. 62
    - 1

4. 55
    - 5

5. 46
    - 3

6. 28
    - 2

7. 97
    - 4

8. 79
    - 6

9. 88
    - 4

10. 29
    - 7

11. 69
    - 2

12. 58
    - 5

Subtracting one-digit numbers from two-digit numbers without regrouping

Subtract Tens from Numbers

Subtract the **ones**.

tens	ones
6	**5**
-4	**0**
	5

Subtract the **tens**.

tens	ones
6	5
-4	0
2	5

Find the **difference**.

1. 43
   - 30
   _____

2. 36
   - 10
   _____

3. 55
   - 50
   _____

4. 97
   - 40
   _____

5. 78
   - 20
   _____

6. 69
   - 50
   _____

7. 84
   - 40
   _____

8. 58
   - 40
   _____

9. 57
   - 20
   _____

10. 41
   - 30
   _____

11. 78
   - 70
   _____

12. 90
   - 90
   _____

Find the **difference**.

13. 67 – 30 = _____

14. 34 – 10 = _____

15. 83 – 50 = _____

16. 42 – 20 = _____

17. 73 – 60 = _____

18. 91 – 60 = _____

Subtracting two-digit numbers without regrouping

Subtract Two-Digit Numbers

Subtract the **ones**.

$$\begin{array}{r} 7\ \textbf{5} \\ -\ 3\ \textbf{4} \\ \hline \textbf{1} \end{array}$$

Subtract the **tens**.

$$\begin{array}{r} \textbf{7}\ 5 \\ -\ \textbf{3}\ 4 \\ \hline \textbf{4}\ 1 \end{array}$$

You can check your answer by adding.

Check

$$\begin{array}{r} 4\ 1 \\ +\ 3\ 4 \\ \hline 7\ 5 \end{array}$$

Find the **difference**. Check your answer.

1.
$$\begin{array}{r} 54 \\ -\ 21 \\ \hline 33 \end{array}$$

Check
$$\begin{array}{r} 33 \\ +\ 21 \\ \hline 54 \end{array}$$

2.
$$\begin{array}{r} 74 \\ -\ 52 \\ \hline \end{array}$$

Check
$$+\ \underline{\qquad}$$

3.
$$\begin{array}{r} 86 \\ -\ 36 \\ \hline \end{array}$$

Check
$$+\ \underline{\qquad}$$

4.
$$\begin{array}{r} 39 \\ -\ 33 \\ \hline \end{array}$$

Check
$$+\ \underline{\qquad}$$

5.
$$\begin{array}{r} 93 \\ -\ 42 \\ \hline \end{array}$$

Check
$$+\ \underline{\qquad}$$

6.
$$\begin{array}{r} 81 \\ -\ 60 \\ \hline \end{array}$$

Check
$$+\ \underline{\qquad}$$

Subtract in Your Head

Subtract to finish the number wheels. Use mental math.

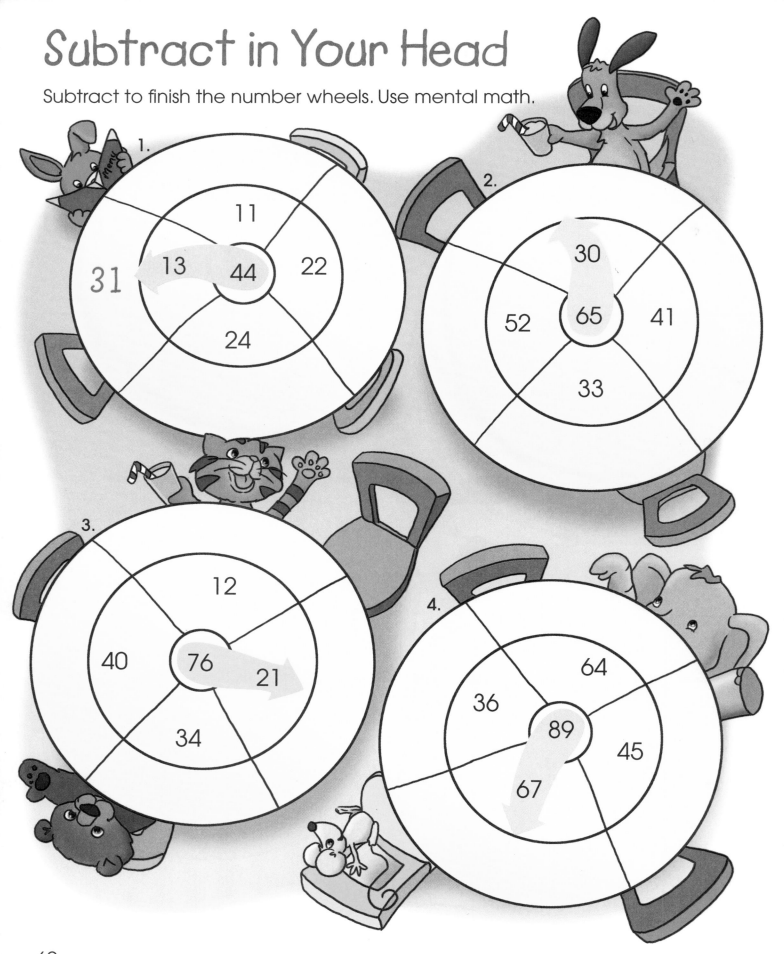

1. 44 — 11, 22, 24, 13 → 31

2. 65 — 30, 41, 33, 52

3. 76 — 12, 21, 34, 40

4. 89 — 64, 45, 67, 36

Find the Sums and Differences

Watch out!
Look for the **+**
and **–** signs.

Find the **sum** or **difference**.

1. 56
    – 25
    ——
    31

2. 29
    + 18
    ——
    47

3. 43
    + 31
    ——
    74

4. 40
    – 12
    ——
    28

5. ³⁴⁵ 45
    – 26
    ——
    19

6. 65
    + 20
    ——
    85

7. 78
    – 28
    ——
    50

8. 73
    + 17
    ——
    90

9. 87
    – 37
    ——
    50

10. ⁴¹³ 53
    – 35
    ——
    18

11. 66
    + 15
    ——
    81

12. 54
    – 44
    ——
    10

13. 39
    + 48
    ——
    87

14. 80
    – 50
    ——
    30

15. 35
    + 27
    ——
    62

16. 49
    – 47
    ——
    2

17. 46
    + 33
    ——
    79

18. ⁷¹⁴ 84
    – 15
    ——
    69

19. 39
    + 29
    ——
    68

20. 53
    + 16
    ——
    69

Adding and subtracting two-digit numbers with regrouping

Solve the Riddle

Solve this riddle:
Which land animal weighs the most?
Add or subtract to find the answer.

F	N	N	C
54 + 18	74 − 7	86 − 9	75 + 6

P	E	A	H
35 + 29	48 + 7	28 − 9	82 − 4

T	E	H	R
39 + 49	39 + 16	85 − 7	47 + 6

A	A	L	I
55 − 36	34 − 15	59 + 7	29 + 68

The ___ ___ ___ ___ ___ ___ ___
19 72 53 97 81 19 67

___ ___ ___ ___ ___ ___ ___ ___
55 66 55 64 78 19 77 88

Two-Digit Number Review

Circle the objects in groups of ten. Write the number of tens and ones. Then write how many there are in all.

1.

_____tens _____ones

How many?_____

2.

_____tens _____ones

How many?_____

Write how many tens and ones there are. Then write the number.

3.

_____tens _____ones = _____

4.

_____tens _____ones = _____

Which number comes **before, between,** or **after?**

5. 63, _____, 65

6. 78, 79, _____

7. _____, 20, 21

8. 39, _____, 41

9. _____, 50, 51

10. 98, 99, _____

Compare the numbers. Then write **<, >,** or **=** in the circle.

11. 28 ◯ 82

12. 64 ◯ 35

13. 73 ◯ 78

14. Circle the **even** numbers.   23   54   60   76   81   49

More Two-Digit Number Review

Write the number or number name.

1. thirty-seven _____

2. 11 _____

3. fifty-three _____

4. 48 _____

Find the **sum** or **difference**.

5. 43
   + 25
   ____

6. 36
   + 9
   ____

7. 54
   + 16
   ____

8. 67
   + 30
   ____

9. 76
   - 40
   ____

10. 81
   - 17
   ____

11. 52
   - 7
   ____

12. 90
   - 56
   ____

13. 25
   + 62
   ____

14. 46
   - 25
   ____

15. 67
   - 18
   ____

16. 73
   + 19
   ____

17. Connect the dots.
    Count by 5s from 5 to 100.

Reviewing two-digit numbers and operations   © School Zone Publishing Company

Tally Charts

A **chart** is a way to show a collection of data.

The data in this chart was recorded using **tally marks**, so this is called a tally chart.

I = 1	HHt = 5
HHt III = 8	

Favorite Foods for Lunch	
Food	Tally
Hamburger	HHt HHt HHt HHt II
Pizza	HHt HHt HHt III
Taco	HHt HHt HHt HHt

Use the tally chart to answer the questions.

1. Copy the tally marks for pizza. _____

   How many children like pizza for lunch? _____

2. How many children like tacos? _____

3. How many children like hamburgers? _____

4. Which food is the favorite? _____

5. How many children like tacos and pizza? _____

6. More children like hamburgers than pizza.
   How many more children like hamburgers? _____

7. How many children were in this survey? _____

Tally Charts

Make a tally chart to record the colors of the birds in the picture.
Then write the total for each.

Bird Color		
Color	Tally	Total
Blue		
Brown		
Red		

Use the tally chart to answer the questions.

1. There are the most of which color bird? _____

2. How many brown and red birds are there? _____

3. There are more blue birds than red birds.
   How many more blue birds are there? _____

4. How many birds are there in all? _____

Tally Charts

Sunflowers Roses Daisies Tulips

Make a tally chart to record the number of flowers in the picture.
Then write the total for each.

Type of Flower	Number of Flowers		
	Tally		Total
Daisy			
Rose			
Tulip			
Sunflower			

Use the tally chart to answer the questions.

1. There are the fewest number of which type of flower? _____

2. How many daisies and sunflowers are there? _____

3. There are more roses than tulips.
   How many more roses are there? _____

4. How many flowers are there in all? _____

Making and interpreting a tally chart

Tally Charts

Baseball Card Collections		
Name	Tally	Total
	~~IIII~~ ~~IIII~~ ~~IIII~~ ~~IIII~~ II	
	~~IIII~~ ~~IIII~~ ~~IIII~~	
		25
Jason		**19**

Use these clues to complete the tally chart:
- John has 22 baseball cards.
- Nick collected more baseball cards than John.
- Alan collected fewer baseball cards than Jason.

Use the tally chart to fill in the blanks in the story.

Alan has _____ baseball cards, and Nick has _____

baseball cards. _____ has the most baseball

cards. Nick and Alan have _____ baseball cards in all.

Nick has _____ more baseball cards than Jason.

Altogether, the boys have _____ baseball cards.

Pictographs

A **pictograph** is a way to show a collection of data.

The data in a pictograph can be recorded using pictures or symbols.

In this pictograph, each 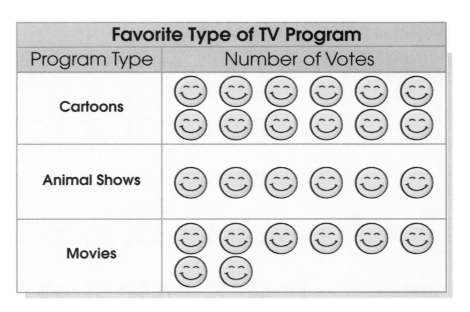 stands for 1 child's vote.

Favorite Type of TV Program	
Program Type	Number of Votes
Cartoons	☺ ☺ ☺ ☺ ☺ ☺ ☺ ☺ ☺ ☺ ☺ ☺
Animal Shows	☺ ☺ ☺ ☺ ☺ ☺
Movies	☺ ☺ ☺ ☺ ☺ ☺ ☺ ☺

Each ☺ = 1 child's vote

Use the pictograph to answer the questions.

1. How many children like animal shows? _____

2. How many children like cartoons? _____

3. How many children like movies? _____

4. Which is the favorite type of TV program? _____

5. More children like cartoons than animal shows. How many more children like cartoons? _____

6. How many children like cartoons and movies? _____

7. How many children were asked about their favorite TV programs? _____

Pictographs

Sticker Collections	
Name	Number of Stickers
Dan	☆ ☆ ☆ ☆ ☆ ☆ ☆ ☆ ☆ ☆ ☆ ☆
Amy	☆ ☆ ☆ ☆ ☆ ☆ ☆ ☆ ☆ ☆ ☆ ☆ ☆ ☆
Jim	☆ ☆ ☆ ☆ ☆ ☆ ☆ ☆ ☆ ☆ ☆
Megan	☆ ☆ ☆ ☆ ☆ ☆ ☆ ☆ ☆ ☆ ☆

Each ☆ = 1 sticker

Use the pictograph to answer the questions.

1. How many stickers does Jim have? _____

2. How many stickers does Dan have? _____

3. How many stickers does Megan have? _____

4. How many stickers does Amy have? _____

5. Who has the fewest stickers? _____

6. Which two children have the same number of stickers?

   _____ and _____

7. How many stickers do Amy and Megan have in all? _____

Pictographs

As you've learned, a **pictograph** is a way to show a collection of data.

In some pictographs, a picture or symbol stands for more than 1 object.

In this pictograph, each 🧦 stands for 2 socks.

Socks in Lost and Found	
Day	Number of Socks
Monday	🧦 🧦 🧦 🧦 🧦
Tuesday	🧦 🧦
Wednesday	🧦 🧦 🧦 🧦 🧦 🧦
Thursday	🧦 🧦 🧦
Friday	🧦 🧦 🧦 🧦

Each 🧦 = 2 socks

Use the pictograph to answer the questions.

1. If 1 🧦 stands for 2 socks, how many socks do 2 🧦s stand for? _____

   3 🧦s? _____   4 🧦s ? _____   5 🧦s ? _____

2. How many socks were there in Lost and Found on Monday? _____

3. How many socks were lost on Friday? _____

4. How many socks were lost on Tuesday? _____

5. More socks were lost on Wednesday than Thursday. How many more socks were lost on Wednesday? _____

6. How can you count the number of socks in the graph quickly?

   _____

Interpreting a pictograph   75

Pictographs

Number of Library Books Read	
Name	Number of Books Read
Tom	📕📕📕
Rosa	📕📕📕📕📕
Justin	📕📕📕📕📕📕📕
Pam	📕📕📕📕

Each 📕 = 5 books

Use the pictograph to answer the questions.

1. What does each 📕 stand for? _____

2. How can you count the number of books in the graph quickly?
    _____

3. How many books did Pam read? _____

4. How many books did Rosa read? _____

5. Who read the most books? _____

6. How many books did Tom and Justin read in all? _____

7. Justin read more books than Rosa.
    How many more books did Justin read? _____

8. How many books did the children read altogether? _____

Pictographs

Stamp Collections										
Name	Number of Stamps									
Jenny	🔲	🔲	🔲	🔲	🔲	🔲	🔲	🔲		
Lisa	🔲	🔲	🔲	🔲	🔲	🔲	🔲	🔲	🔲	🔲
Jose	🔲	🔲	🔲	🔲	🔲	🔲	🔲	🔲	🔲	
Ray	🔲	🔲	🔲	🔲	🔲	🔲				

Each  = 2 stamps

Use the pictograph to answer the questions.

1. What does each 🔲 stand for? _____

2. How can you count the number of stamps in the graph quickly?

   _____

3. How many stamps does Jose have? _____

4. How many stamps does Jenny have? _____

5. Who has the most stamps? _____

6. Who has fewer stamps than Jenny? _____

7. Lisa has more stamps than Jenny.
   How many more stamps does Lisa have? _____

Bar Graphs

A **bar graph** is a way to show a collection of data.

A bar graph uses bars to record data.

Read the number at the end of the bar to tell how many.

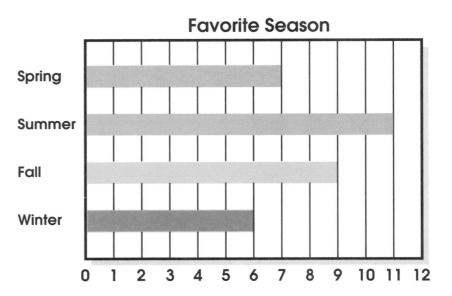

Favorite Season

Spring
Summer
Fall
Winter

0 1 2 3 4 5 6 7 8 9 10 11 12

Use the bar graph to answer the questions.

1. How many children like winter best? _____

2. How many children like spring best? _____

3. How many children like fall best? _____

4. Which season is the favorite? _____

5. Which season is the least favorite? _____

6. More children like summer than spring.
   How many more children like summer? _____

Bar Graphs

Read the number at the top of the bar to tell how many.

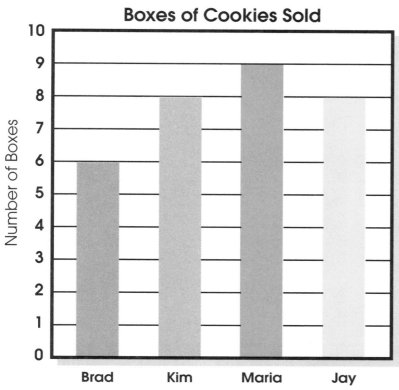

Boxes of Cookies Sold

Use the bar graph to answer the questions.

1. How many boxes of cookies did Kim sell? _____

2. How many boxes did Maria sell? _____

3. How many boxes did Brad sell? _____

4. Who sold the most boxes? _____

5. Who sold the fewest boxes? _____

6. Which two children sold the same number of boxes?

   _____ and _____

7. How many boxes did the children sell in all? _____

Bar Graphs

As you've learned, a **bar graph** is a way to show a collection of data.

To show larger amounts of things, the numbers on the side of a bar graph use greater numbers.

Favorite Juices

Number of Children

20
18
16
14
12
10
8
6
4
2
0

Apple   Orange   Grape   Tomato

Use the bar graph to answer the questions.

1. How many children like tomato juice? _____

2. How many children like apple juice? _____

3. Which juice is the favorite? _____
   How many children like it? _____

4. Which juice is the least favorite? _____
   How many children like it? _____

5. More children like orange juice than tomato juice.
   How many more children like orange juice? _____

6. How many children like apple juice and grape juice in all? _____

7. Are there more than or less than 50 children in this survey? _____

Bar Graphs

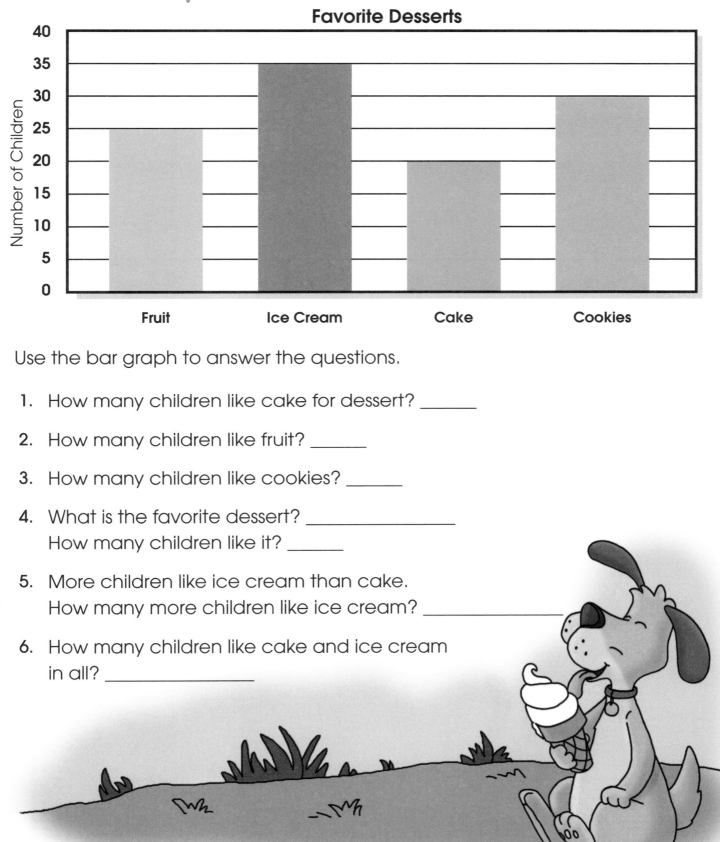

Favorite Desserts

Number of Children

40 · 35 · 30 · 25 · 20 · 15 · 10 · 5 · 0

Fruit   Ice Cream   Cake   Cookies

Use the bar graph to answer the questions.

1. How many children like cake for dessert? _____

2. How many children like fruit? _____

3. How many children like cookies? _____

4. What is the favorite dessert? _____
   How many children like it? _____

5. More children like ice cream than cake.
   How many more children like ice cream? _____

6. How many children like cake and ice cream
   in all? _____

Bar Graphs

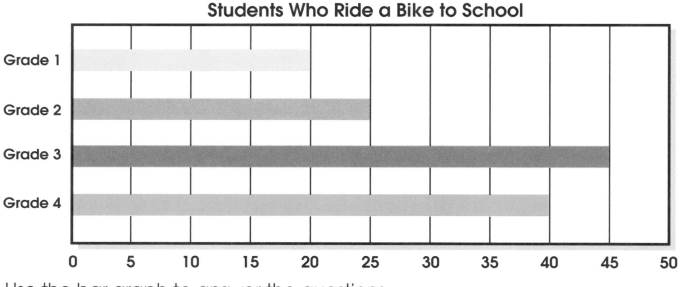

Students Who Ride a Bike to School

Use the bar graph to answer the questions.

1. How many children in grade 2 ride a bike to school? _____

2. How many children in grade 4 ride a bike to school? _____

3. Which grade has the most bike riders? _____
   How many bike riders are there? _____

4. How many children in grades 1 and 2 ride a bike to school? _____

5. How many more children in grade 3 ride a bike to school than
   in grade 1? _____

6. Are there more than or less than 50 bike riders in grades 1 and 2? _____

Tables

A **table** is a way to show a collection of data.

Favorite Color	
Color	Number of Votes
Red	17
Blue	20
Green	15
Purple	10

Use the table to answer the questions.

1. How many children like the color green? _____

2. How many children like purple? _____

3. How many children like red? _____

4. Which color is the favorite? _____

5. Which color is the least favorite? _____

6. How many children like blue and green in all? _____

7. More children like red than purple.
    How many more children like red? _____

Tables

Favorite Season		
Season	Number of Votes in Grade 2	Number of Votes in Grade 3
Spring	28	34
Summer	40	38
Fall	32	29
Winter	17	22

Use the table to answer the questions.

1. How many children in grade 2 like summer best? _____

2. How many children in grade 3 like summer best? _____

3. How many children in grade 3 like winter best? _____

4. How many children in grade 2 like fall best? _____

5. Which season do children in grade 3 like best? _____

6. Which season do children in grade 2 like least? _____

Hundreds

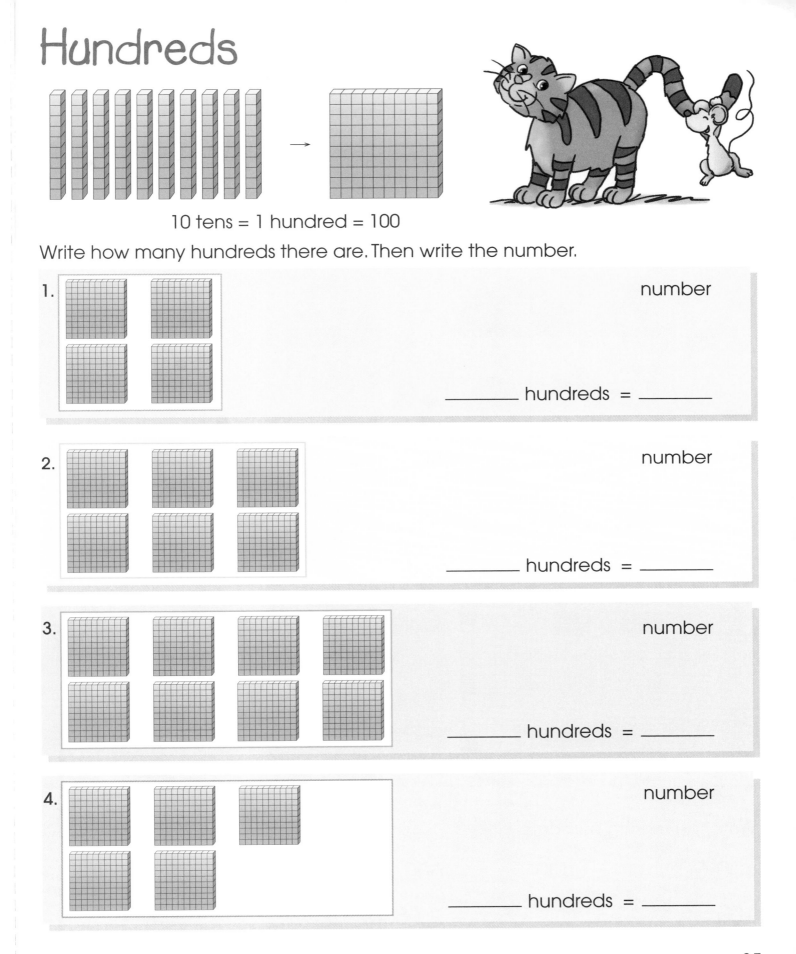

10 tens = 1 hundred = 100

Write how many hundreds there are. Then write the number.

1.

number

_____ hundreds = _____

2.

number

_____ hundreds = _____

3.

number

_____ hundreds = _____

4.

number

_____ hundreds = _____

Count by Hundreds

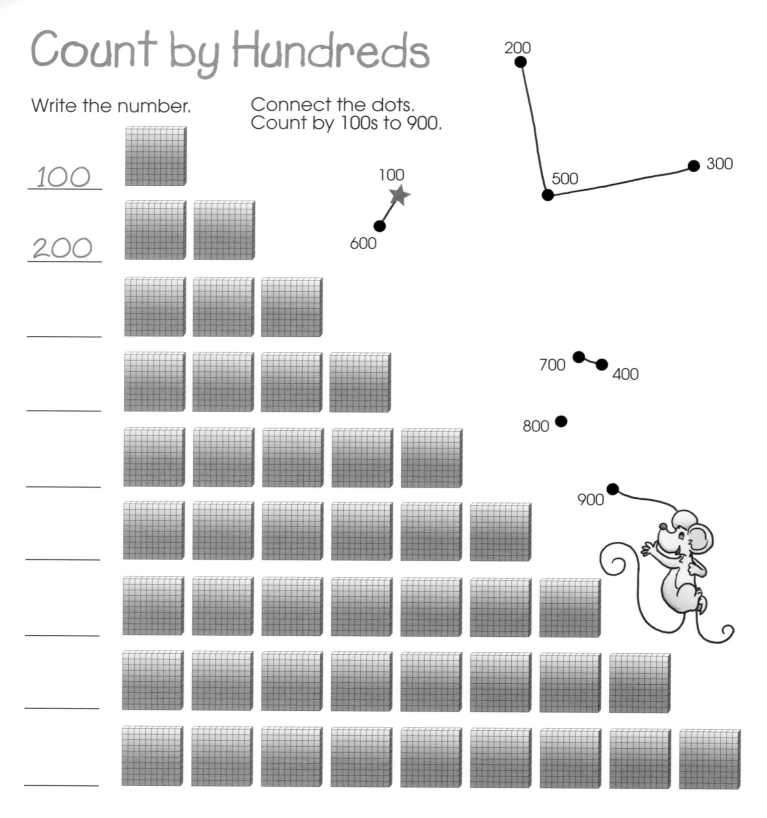

Write the number.

100

200

_____

_____

_____

_____

_____

_____

Connect the dots.
Count by 100s to 900.

Write the missing numbers.

100, 200, _____ , 400, _____ , 600, _____ , 800, _____

100, _____ , 300, _____ , _____ , 600, _____ , _____ , 900

Hundreds, Tens, and Ones

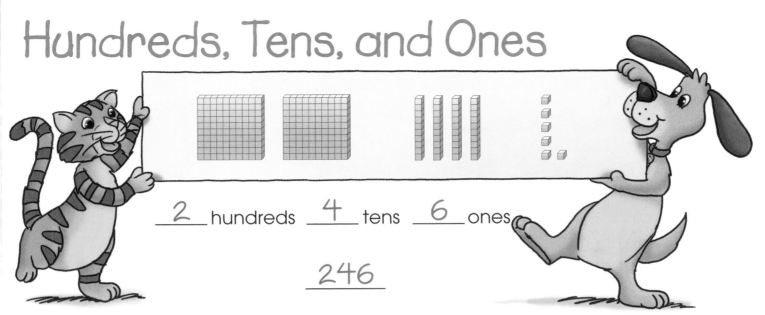

___2___ hundreds ___4___ tens ___6___ ones

___246___

Write how many hundreds, tens, and ones there are.
Then write the number.

1.

_____ hundreds _____ tens _____ ones

_____

2.

_____ hundreds _____ tens _____ ones

_____

3.

_____ hundreds _____ tens _____ ones

_____

4.

_____ hundreds _____ tens _____ ones

_____

Match Greater Numbers

Match each group to the correct number.

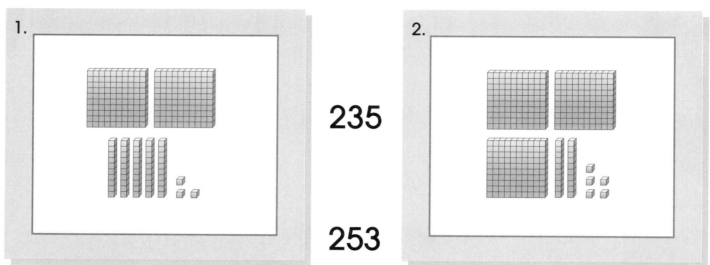

1.

235

253

2.

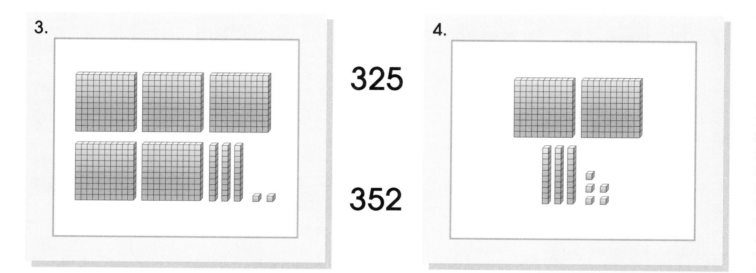

3.

325

352

4.

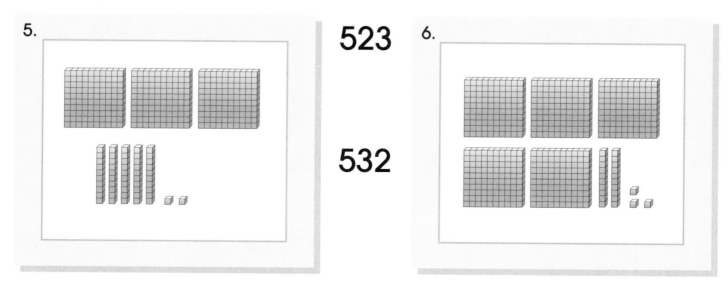

5.

523

532

6.

Understanding three-digit numbers

Find the Hundreds

$$296 = 2 \overset{\text{hundreds}}{2} \overset{\text{tens}}{9} \overset{\text{ones}}{6}$$

Read the question.
Circle the correct answer.

1. Which number shows 4 hundreds?   324   (422)   243

2. Which number shows 2 hundreds?   280   120   342

3. Which number shows 8 hundreds?   618   580   800

4. Which number shows 5 hundreds?   125   251   512

5. Which number shows 1 hundred?   180   801   810

6. Which number shows 9 hundreds?   490   966   489

7. Which number shows 3 hundreds?   324   833   133

8. Which number shows 6 hundreds?   465   678   396

9. Which number shows 7 hundreds?   700   570   897

10. Which number shows 5 hundreds?   205   355   555

11. Which number shows 0 hundreds?   180   510   90

12. Which number shows 9 hundreds?   192   944   899

13. **Challenge:** Make as many numbers as you can from these digits: 2, 5, and 8. Use one, two, or all three digits to make a number.

Making more than 10 numbers is great!

Understanding place value of three-digit numbers

Find the Hundreds, Tens, and Ones

Read the problem.
Circle the correct digit in the number.

1. Circle the hundreds. 4 8 7
2. Circle the ones. 2 8 9
3. Circle the hundreds. 3 3 3
4. Circle the tens. 8 2 5
5. Circle the tens. 4 0 0
6. Circle the hundreds. 8 9 9
7. Circle the hundreds. 2 1 5
8. Circle the tens. 4 5 8
9. Circle the ones. 5 7 0
10. Circle the ones. 8 6 7
11. Circle the hundreds. 6 4 8
12. Circle the tens. 4 4 4

13. Circle Hanna's house number. It has **7** hundreds and **9** tens.

7 8 5   9 7 6   7 6 5   9 9 7   7 9 6

Count by Hundreds, Tens, and Ones

Connect the dots.
Start at the ▲ and count by 100s to 900.
Start at the ● and count by 10s to 290.
Start at the ■ and count by 1s from 451 to 470.

Which Numbers Are Missing?

Write the missing numbers.

1. 100, 101, _____, 103, _____, 105

2. 215, _____, 217, _____, 219, _____

3. 746, _____, 748, 749, _____, 751

4. 505, 510, _____, 520, _____, _____

5. 300, _____, _____, 600, _____, 800

6. 410, _____, 430, _____, 450, _____

7. 645, _____, 655, 660, _____, _____

Before, Between, and After

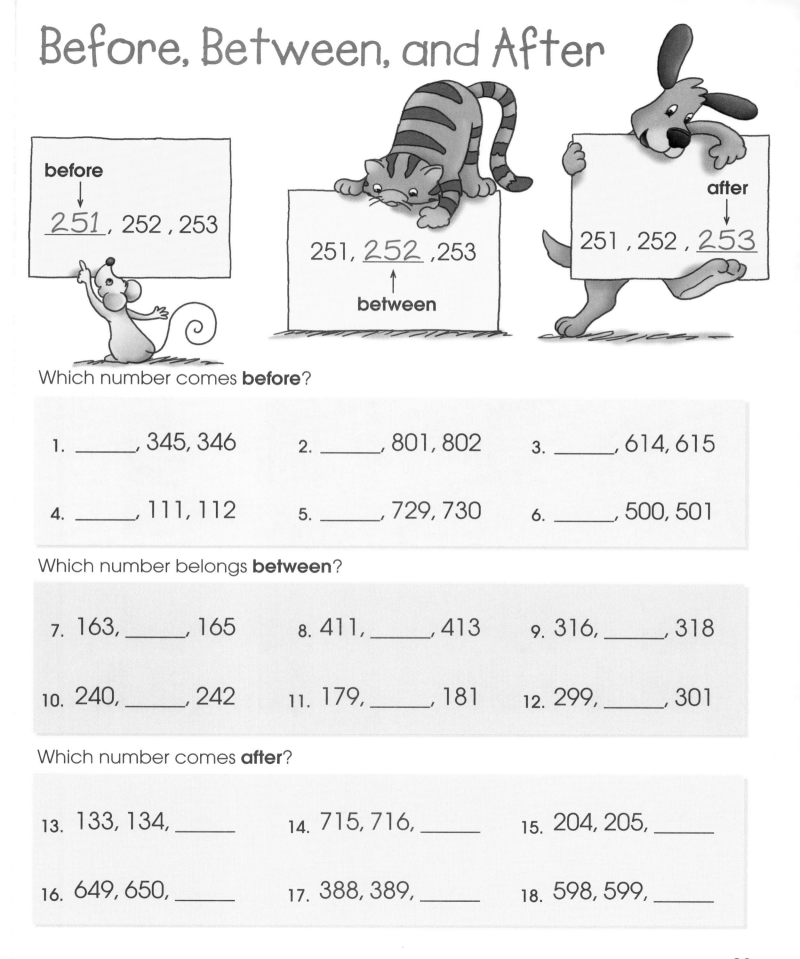

before
↓
251 , 252 , 253

251, **252** ,253
↑
between

after
↓
251 , 252 , **253**

Which number comes **before**?

1. _____ , 345, 346

2. _____ , 801, 802

3. _____ , 614, 615

4. _____ , 111, 112

5. _____ , 729, 730

6. _____ , 500, 501

Which number belongs **between**?

7. 163, _____ , 165

8. 411, _____ , 413

9. 316, _____ , 318

10. 240, _____ , 242

11. 179, _____ , 181

12. 299, _____ , 301

Which number comes **after**?

13. 133, 134, _____

14. 715, 716, _____

15. 204, 205, _____

16. 649, 650, _____

17. 388, 389, _____

18. 598, 599, _____

Concepts of *before, between,* and *after*

Compare Numbers

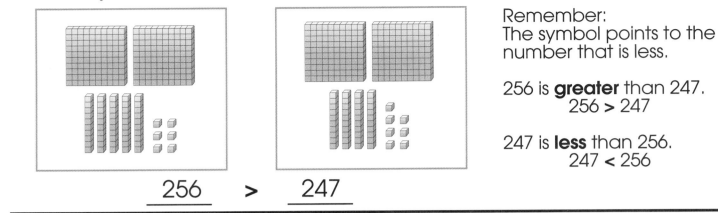

Remember:
The symbol points to the number that is less.

256 is **greater** than 247.
256 > 247

247 is **less** than 256.
247 < 256

256 > 247

Write the numbers. Compare the numbers.
Then write <, >, or = in the ◯ .

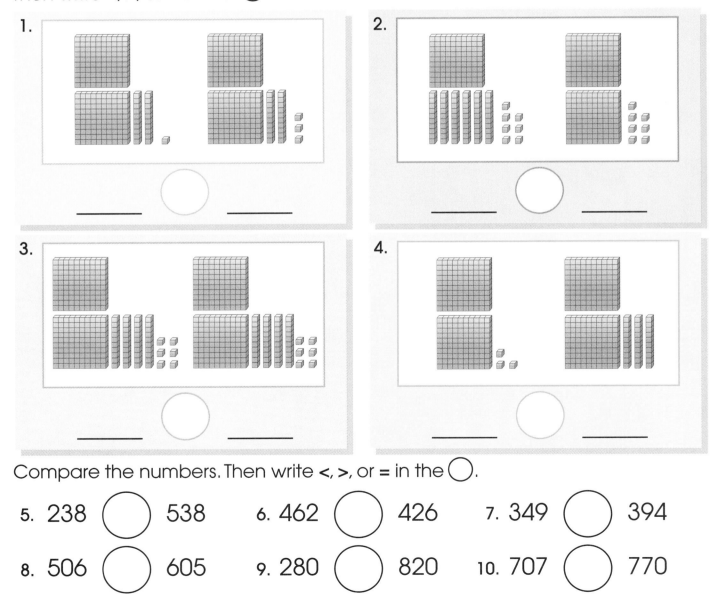

Compare the numbers. Then write <, >, or = in the ◯.

5. 238 ◯ 538   6. 462 ◯ 426   7. 349 ◯ 394

8. 506 ◯ 605   9. 280 ◯ 820   10. 707 ◯ 770

Greater or Less

Look at the hundreds digits in both numbers first and compare.
If the hundreds digits are the same, look at the tens digits.
If the hundreds and tens digits are the same, look at the ones digits.

Compare the hundreds.

437   399

greater less

437 has
more hundreds.

Compare the tens.

347   352

less   greater

352 has
more tens.

Compare the ones.

437   439

less   greater

439 has
more ones.

Circle the number that is **greater**.

1. 365 368   2. 574 584   3. 309 903

4. 700 170   5. 252 262   6. 878 788

7. 640 639   8. 901 910   9. 565 562

Circle the number that is **less**.

10. 770 790   11. 418 480   12. 620 532

13. 765 791   14. 943 948   15. 730 639

16. 391 399   17. 707 609   18. 828 728

Least to Greatest

Write the numbers in order from **least** to **greatest**.

1. 327   392   329

_____

2. 701   107   170

_____

3. 535   553   355

_____

4. 671   618   617

_____

5. 432   437   434

_____

6. 264   282   273

_____

7. 901   911   191

_____

8. 498   490   489

_____

9. 883   858   839

_____

10. 351   393   319

_____

Find Greater Sums

When you add two-digit numbers, sometimes the sum is a three-digit number.

$$\begin{array}{r} 76 \\ + 53 \\ \hline 129 \end{array}$$

Find the **sum**. Regroup if needed.

1. $\begin{array}{r} 65 \\ + 52 \\ \hline 117 \end{array}$

2. $\begin{array}{r} 53 \\ + 56 \\ \hline 109 \end{array}$

3. $\begin{array}{r} 47 \\ + 85 \\ \hline 132 \end{array}$

4. $\begin{array}{r} 93 \\ + 28 \\ \hline 121 \end{array}$

5. $\begin{array}{r} 95 \\ + 12 \\ \hline 107 \end{array}$

6. $\begin{array}{r} 82 \\ + 28 \\ \hline 110 \end{array}$

7. $\begin{array}{r} 63 \\ + 37 \\ \hline 100 \end{array}$

8. $\begin{array}{r} 75 \\ + 75 \\ \hline 150 \end{array}$

9. $\begin{array}{r} 90 \\ + 46 \\ \hline 136 \end{array}$

10. $\begin{array}{r} 88 \\ + 88 \\ \hline 176 \end{array}$

11. $\begin{array}{r} 91 \\ + 19 \\ \hline 110 \end{array}$

12. $\begin{array}{r} 73 \\ + 38 \\ \hline 111 \end{array}$

13. $\begin{array}{r} 94 \\ + 49 \\ \hline 143 \end{array}$

14. $\begin{array}{r} 76 \\ + 45 \\ \hline 121 \end{array}$

15. $\begin{array}{r} 57 \\ + 75 \\ \hline 132 \end{array}$

16. $\begin{array}{r} 91 \\ + 29 \\ \hline 120 \end{array}$

Adding two-digit numbers; sums greater than 100

Add More Numbers

Let's add these numbers:

53 + 84 + 9

To check your answer,
add the numbers
in the opposite order.

$$\begin{array}{r} {}^1\ 53 \\ 84 \\ +\ \ 9 \\ \hline 146 \end{array}$$

$$\begin{array}{r} {}^1 9 \\ 84 \\ +\ 53 \\ \hline 146 \end{array}$$

Find the **sum**. Regroup if needed.

1.
$$\begin{array}{r} 32 \\ 21 \\ +\ 15 \\ \hline 68 \end{array}$$

2.
$$\begin{array}{r} 63 \\ 12 \\ +\ 44 \\ \hline 119 \end{array}$$

3.
$$\begin{array}{r} {}^1 73 \\ 6 \\ +\ 25 \\ \hline 104 \end{array}$$

4.
$$\begin{array}{r} {}^2 97 \\ 98 \\ +\ 99 \\ \hline 294 \end{array}$$

5.
$$\begin{array}{r} {}^1 12 \\ 14 \\ 15 \\ +\ 18 \\ \hline 59 \end{array}$$

6.
$$\begin{array}{r} {}^1 45 \\ 21 \\ 30 \\ +\ 24 \\ \hline 120 \end{array}$$

7.
$$\begin{array}{r} {}^1 64 \\ 8 \\ 37 \\ +\ 40 \\ \hline 149 \end{array}$$

8.
$$\begin{array}{r} {}^2 56 \\ 55 \\ 4 \\ +\ 8 \\ \hline 123 \end{array}$$

9. 43 + 6 + 50 = 99

10. 78 + 31 + 88 = _____

11. 65 + 35 + 68 = _____

12. 37 + 8 + 39 = _____

13. 25 + 12 + 31 + 20 = _____

14. 40 + 50 + 60 + 70 = 220

15. 76 + 43 + 5 + 22 = _____

16. 25 + 35 + 45 + 55 = _____

17. This one is a challenge! 12 + 23 + 34 + 45 + 56 + 67 + 78 + 89 = _____

Add with Hundreds

Add the ones. Regroup if needed. | Add the tens. Regroup if needed. | Add the hundreds.

$$
\begin{array}{r}
\overset{1}{3}09 \\
+ 473 \\
\hline
2
\end{array}
\qquad
\begin{array}{r}
\overset{1}{3}09 \\
+ 473 \\
\hline
82
\end{array}
\qquad
\begin{array}{r}
\overset{1}{3}09 \\
+ 473 \\
\hline
782
\end{array}
$$

Find the **sum**. Regroup if needed.

1. $\begin{array}{r} 462 \\ + 321 \\ \hline 783 \end{array}$
2. $\begin{array}{r} 706 \\ + 132 \\ \hline 838 \end{array}$
3. $\begin{array}{r} 450 \\ + 209 \\ \hline 659 \end{array}$
4. $\begin{array}{r} 456 \\ + 123 \\ \hline 579 \end{array}$

5. $\begin{array}{r} 366 \\ + 128 \\ \hline 494 \end{array}$
6. $\begin{array}{r} 572 \\ + 309 \\ \hline 881 \end{array}$
7. $\begin{array}{r} 278 \\ + 329 \\ \hline 607 \end{array}$
8. $\begin{array}{r} 293 \\ + 275 \\ \hline 568 \end{array}$

9. $\begin{array}{r} 435 \\ + \ 48 \\ \hline 483 \end{array}$
10. $\begin{array}{r} 845 \\ + \ 17 \\ \hline 862 \end{array}$
11. $\begin{array}{r} 670 \\ + \ 45 \\ \hline 715 \end{array}$
12. $\begin{array}{r} 777 \\ + \ 19 \\ \hline 796 \end{array}$

These are a challenge!

13. $\begin{array}{r} 352 \\ + 169 \\ \hline 531 \end{array}$
14. $\begin{array}{r} 255 \\ + 355 \\ \hline 610 \end{array}$
15. $\begin{array}{r} 675 \\ + 125 \\ \hline 800 \end{array}$
16. $\begin{array}{r} 456 \\ + 345 \\ \hline 801 \end{array}$

Add Three-Digit Numbers

$$\begin{array}{r} 1 \\ 593 \\ +246 \\ \hline 839 \end{array}$$

Find the **sum**. Regroup if needed.

1. $\begin{array}{r} 188 \\ +\ 10 \\ \hline \end{array}$
2. $\begin{array}{r} 244 \\ +\ 23 \\ \hline \end{array}$
3. $\begin{array}{r} 852 \\ +\ 34 \\ \hline \end{array}$
4. $\begin{array}{r} 205 \\ +\ 41 \\ \hline \end{array}$

5. $\begin{array}{r} 428 \\ +\ 23 \\ \hline \end{array}$
6. $\begin{array}{r} 107 \\ +\ 10 \\ \hline \end{array}$
7. $\begin{array}{r} 314 \\ +\ 48 \\ \hline \end{array}$
8. $\begin{array}{r} 239 \\ +\ 25 \\ \hline \end{array}$

9. $\begin{array}{r} 132 \\ +400 \\ \hline \end{array}$
10. $\begin{array}{r} 135 \\ +\ 37 \\ \hline \end{array}$
11. $\begin{array}{r} 650 \\ +125 \\ \hline \end{array}$
12. $\begin{array}{r} 175 \\ +200 \\ \hline \end{array}$

13. $\begin{array}{r} 125 \\ +470 \\ \hline \end{array}$
14. $\begin{array}{r} 447 \\ +\ 38 \\ \hline \end{array}$
15. $\begin{array}{r} 436 \\ +\ 45 \\ \hline \end{array}$
16. $\begin{array}{r} 546 \\ +137 \\ \hline \end{array}$

It's a breeze!

Subtract with Hundreds

Subtract the **ones**. Regroup if needed.	Subtract the **tens**. Regroup if needed.	Subtract the **hundreds**.	Check
$\begin{array}{r} ^{6}\ ^{13} \\ 57\cancel{3} \\ -\ 206 \\ \hline 7 \end{array}$	$\begin{array}{r} ^{6}\ ^{13} \\ 5\cancel{7}\cancel{3} \\ -\ 206 \\ \hline 67 \end{array}$	$\begin{array}{r} ^{6}\ ^{13} \\ \cancel{5}\cancel{7}\cancel{3} \\ -\ 206 \\ \hline 367 \end{array}$	$\begin{array}{r} ^{1}\quad \\ 367 \\ +\ 206 \\ \hline 573 \end{array}$

Find the **difference**. Regroup if needed.
Check your answer.

Check

1. $\begin{array}{r} 863 \\ -\ 240 \\ \hline \end{array}$ $+\ \rule{3cm}{0.4pt}$

2. $\begin{array}{r} 478 \\ -\ 435 \\ \hline \end{array}$ $+\ \rule{3cm}{0.4pt}$

Check

Check

3. $\begin{array}{r} 573 \\ -\ \ 47 \\ \hline \end{array}$ $+\ \rule{3cm}{0.4pt}$

4. $\begin{array}{r} 350 \\ -\ \ 38 \\ \hline \end{array}$ $+\ \rule{3cm}{0.4pt}$

Check

Check

5. $\begin{array}{r} 851 \\ -\ 316 \\ \hline \end{array}$ $+\ \rule{3cm}{0.4pt}$

6. $\begin{array}{r} 617 \\ -\ 395 \\ \hline \end{array}$ $+\ \rule{3cm}{0.4pt}$

Check

Check

Subtract Three-Digit Numbers

$$\begin{array}{r} {\scriptstyle 6\ 17} \\ 4\cancel{7}\cancel{7} \\ -\ 248 \\ \hline 229 \end{array}$$

Find the **difference**. Regroup if needed.

1. $\begin{array}{r} 146 \\ -\ 22 \\ \hline \end{array}$ 2. $\begin{array}{r} 813 \\ -\ 12 \\ \hline \end{array}$ 3. $\begin{array}{r} 486 \\ -\ 74 \\ \hline \end{array}$ 4. $\begin{array}{r} 333 \\ -\ 12 \\ \hline \end{array}$

5. $\begin{array}{r} 750 \\ -\ 400 \\ \hline \end{array}$ 6. $\begin{array}{r} 681 \\ -\ 351 \\ \hline \end{array}$ 7. $\begin{array}{r} 175 \\ -\ 114 \\ \hline \end{array}$ 8. $\begin{array}{r} 926 \\ -\ 422 \\ \hline \end{array}$

9. $\begin{array}{r} 487 \\ -\ 29 \\ \hline \end{array}$ 10. $\begin{array}{r} 593 \\ -\ 162 \\ \hline \end{array}$ 11. $\begin{array}{r} 296 \\ -\ 89 \\ \hline \end{array}$ 12. $\begin{array}{r} 758 \\ -\ 135 \\ \hline \end{array}$

13. $\begin{array}{r} 832 \\ -\ 109 \\ \hline \end{array}$ 14. $\begin{array}{r} 485 \\ -\ 368 \\ \hline \end{array}$ 15. $\begin{array}{r} 398 \\ -\ 250 \\ \hline \end{array}$ 16. $\begin{array}{r} 459 \\ -\ 47 \\ \hline \end{array}$

Solve the Riddle

Solve this riddle:
Which bird is very sad?
Add and subtract to find the answer.

B	A	E
126	136	351
+ 94	− 75	+123

I	L	W
583	654	345
−516	+ 70	− 139

U	F	B
345	350	664
− 17	+409	+ 11

R	D	C
665	543	678
− 8	+ 37	+200

61   220   724   328   474   675   67   657   580

Addition and Subtraction Puzzle

Add or subtract to complete the puzzle.

Across

1.
$$\begin{array}{r} 65 \\ + 56 \\ \hline \end{array}$$

4.
$$\begin{array}{r} 396 \\ - 125 \\ \hline \end{array}$$

7.
$$\begin{array}{r} 634 \\ + 72 \\ \hline \end{array}$$

8.
$$\begin{array}{r} 487 \\ - 444 \\ \hline \end{array}$$

9.
$$\begin{array}{r} 560 \\ + 129 \\ \hline \end{array}$$

10.
$$\begin{array}{r} 327 \\ - 253 \\ \hline \end{array}$$

12.
$$\begin{array}{r} 695 \\ - 225 \\ \hline \end{array}$$

13.
$$\begin{array}{r} 709 \\ + 204 \\ \hline \end{array}$$

Down

2.
$$\begin{array}{r} 183 \\ + 95 \\ \hline \end{array}$$

3.
$$\begin{array}{r} 578 \\ - 469 \\ \hline \end{array}$$

5.
$$\begin{array}{r} 338 \\ + 406 \\ \hline \end{array}$$

6.
$$\begin{array}{r} 765 \\ - 630 \\ \hline \end{array}$$

9.
$$\begin{array}{r} 440 \\ + 214 \\ \hline \end{array}$$

11.
$$\begin{array}{r} 360 \\ - 311 \\ \hline \end{array}$$

Introduction to Multiplication

Multiplication is a short way to add groups of equal size.

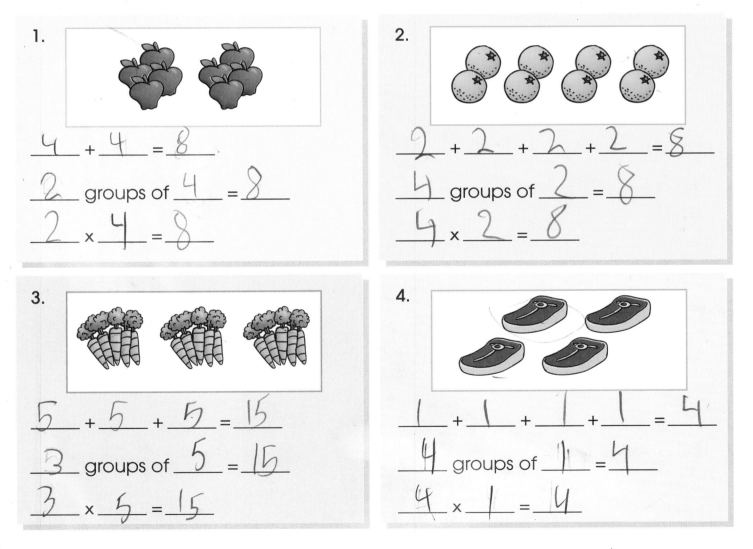

You can add: __2__ + __2__ + __2__ = __6__

Meaning: __3__ groups of __2__ = __6__

You can multiply: __3__ x __2__ = __6__

Fill in the blanks to finish the addition and multiplication sentences.

1.
__4__ + __4__ = __8__
__2__ groups of __4__ = __8__
__2__ x __4__ = __8__

2.
__2__ + __2__ + __2__ + __2__ = __8__
__4__ groups of __2__ = __8__
__4__ x __2__ = __8__

3.
__5__ + __5__ + __5__ = __15__
__3__ groups of __5__ = __15__
__3__ x __5__ = __15__

4.
__1__ + __1__ + __1__ + __1__ = __4__
__4__ groups of __1__ = __4__
__4__ x __1__ = __4__

Multiplication and Addition

4 + 4 + 4 = 12

How many **4**s? ___3___

___3___ x ___4___ = ___12___

6 + 6 + 6 + 6 = 24

How many **6**s? ___4___

___4___ x ___6___ = ___24___

Fill in the blanks to finish the addition and multiplication sentences.

1. 2 + 2 + 2 + 2 = ___

   ___ x ___ = ___

2. 3 + 3 + 3 + 3 = _12_

   ___4___ x ___3___ = _12_

3. 5 + 5 + 5 + 5 + 5 = _25_

   _5_ x _5_ = _25_

4. 4 + 4 + 4 = _12_

   _3_ x _4_ = _12_

5. 1 + 1 + 1 + 1 + 1 = _5_

   _5_ x _1_ = _5_

6. 5 + 5 + 5 = _15_

   _3_ x _5_ = _15_

7. 3 + 3 + 3 = ___

   ___ x ___ = ___

8. 4 + 4 + 4 + 4 = ___

   ___ x ___ = ___

Multiplication and Groups

How many groups are there? __5__

How many s are in each group? __2__

How many s ? __10__

__5__ x __2__ = __10__

Fill in the blanks.

1.

How many groups are there? __4__

How many s are in each group? __2__

How many s ? __8__

__4__ x __2__ = __8__

2.

How many groups are there? __3__

How many s are in each group? __5__

How many s ? __15__

__3__ x __35__ = __15__

Multiplication and Groups

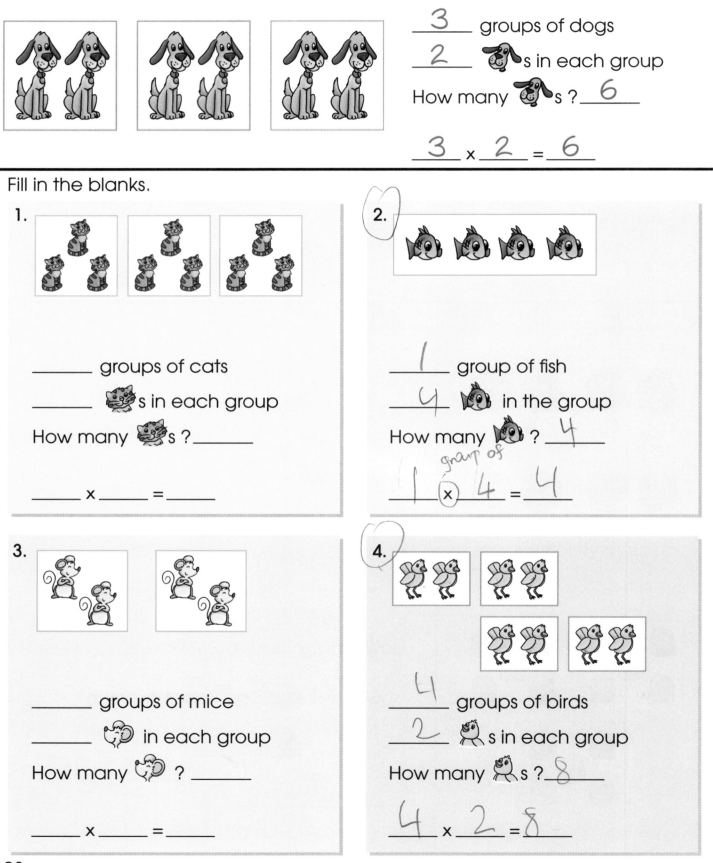

____3____ groups of dogs

____2____ 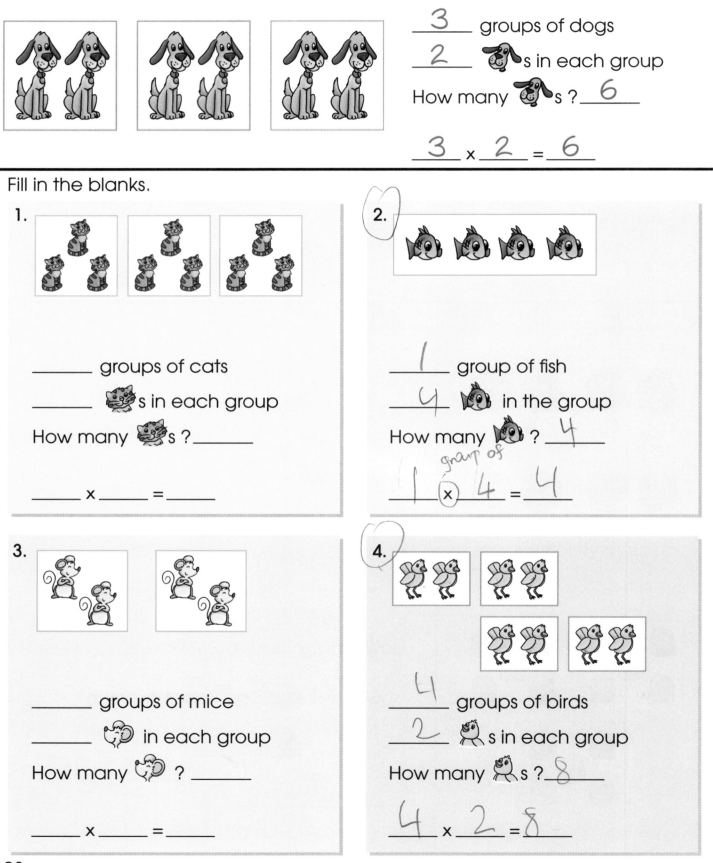s in each group

How many 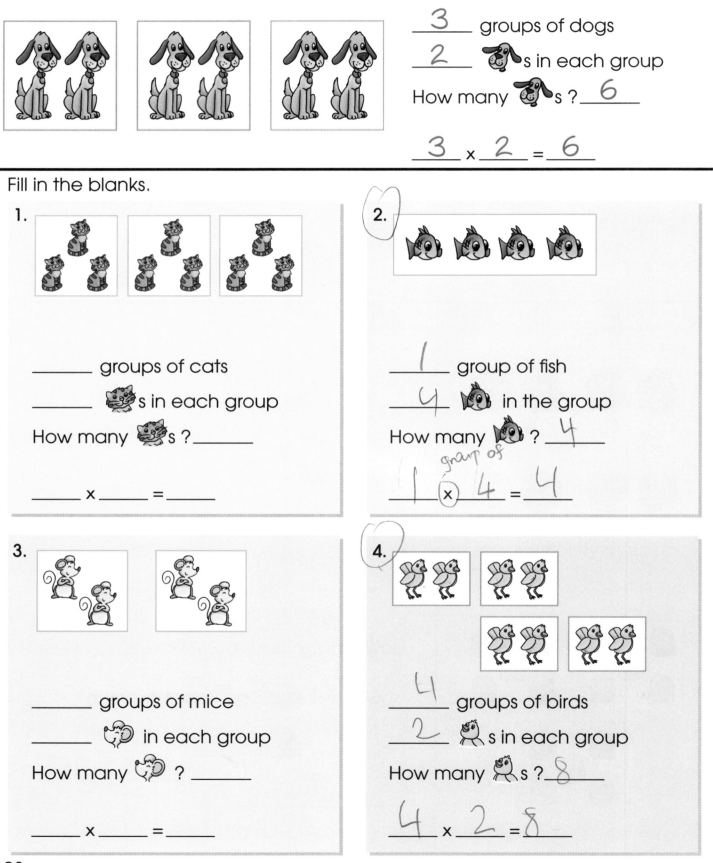s ? ___6___

___3___ x ___2___ = ___6___

Fill in the blanks.

1.

_____ groups of cats

_____ 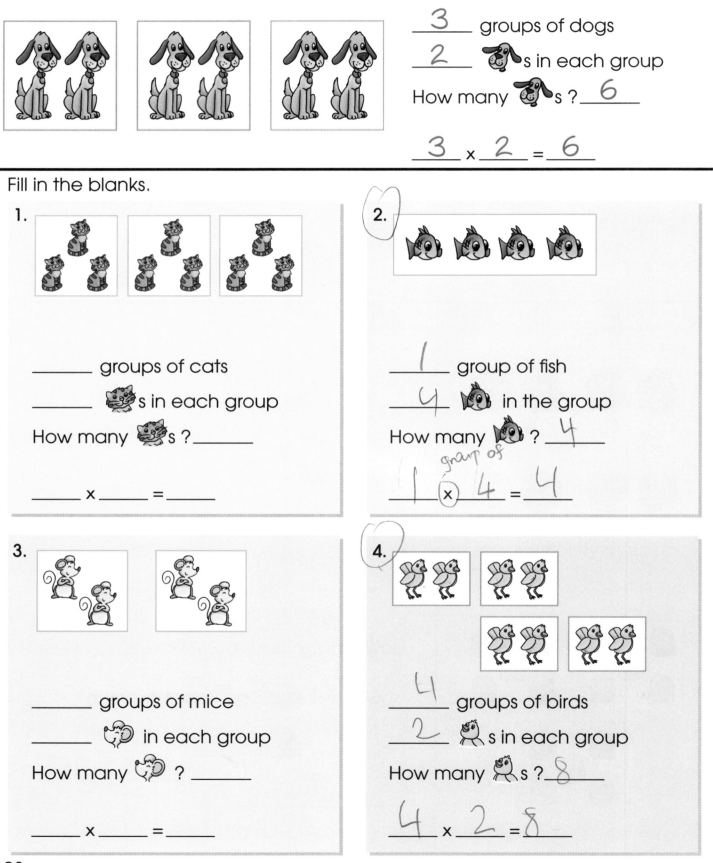s in each group

How many 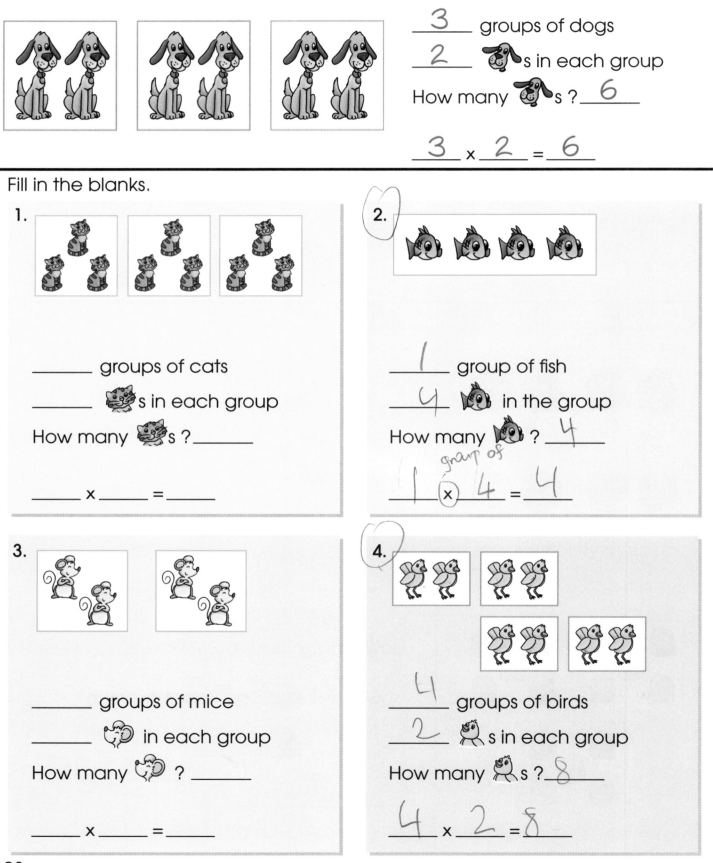s ? _____

_____ x _____ = _____

2.

____1____ group of fish

____4____ 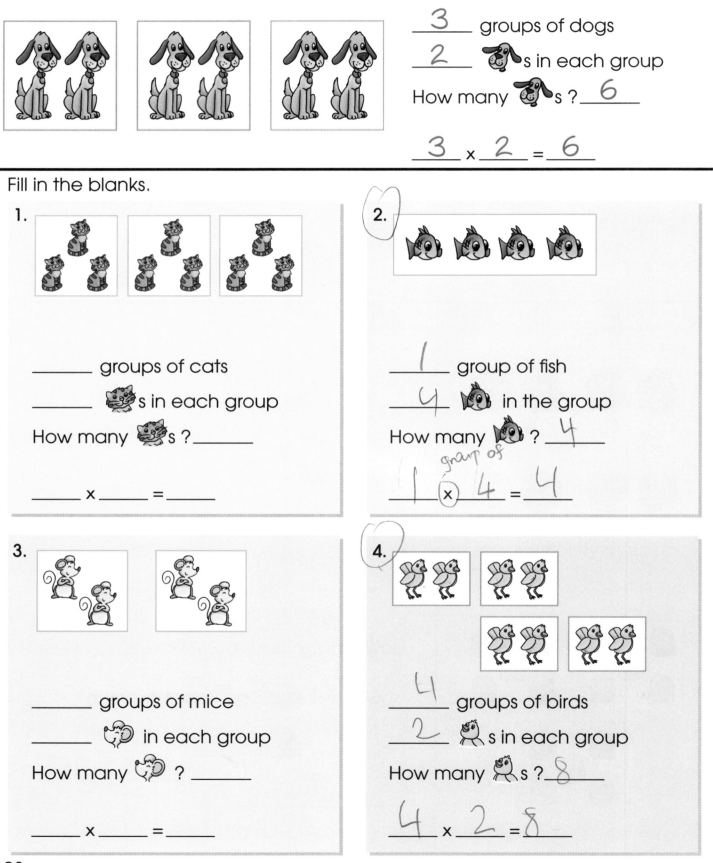 in the group

How many 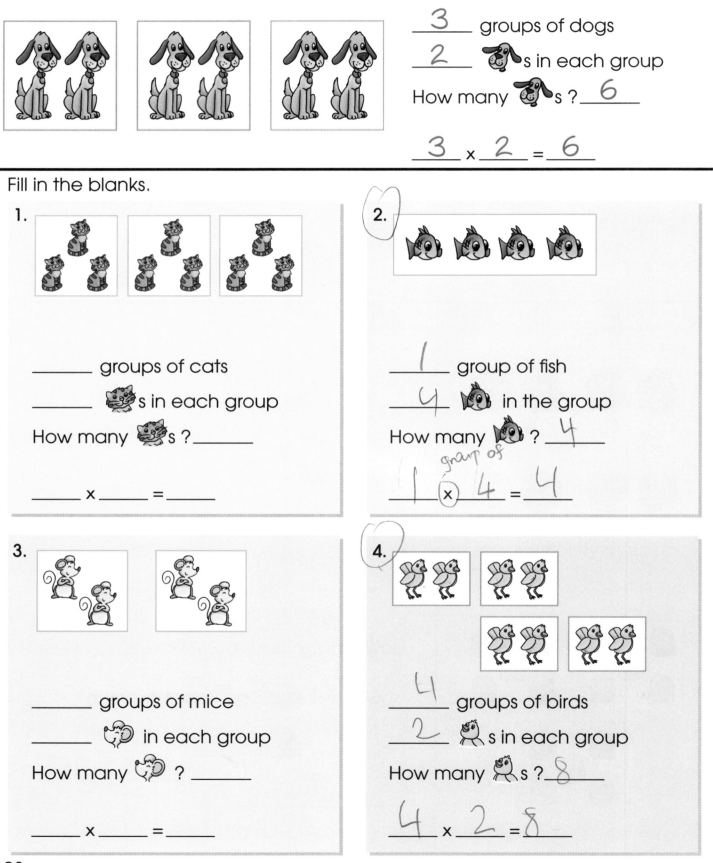 ? ___4___

group of

___1___ (x) ___4___ = _____

3.

_____ groups of mice

_____ 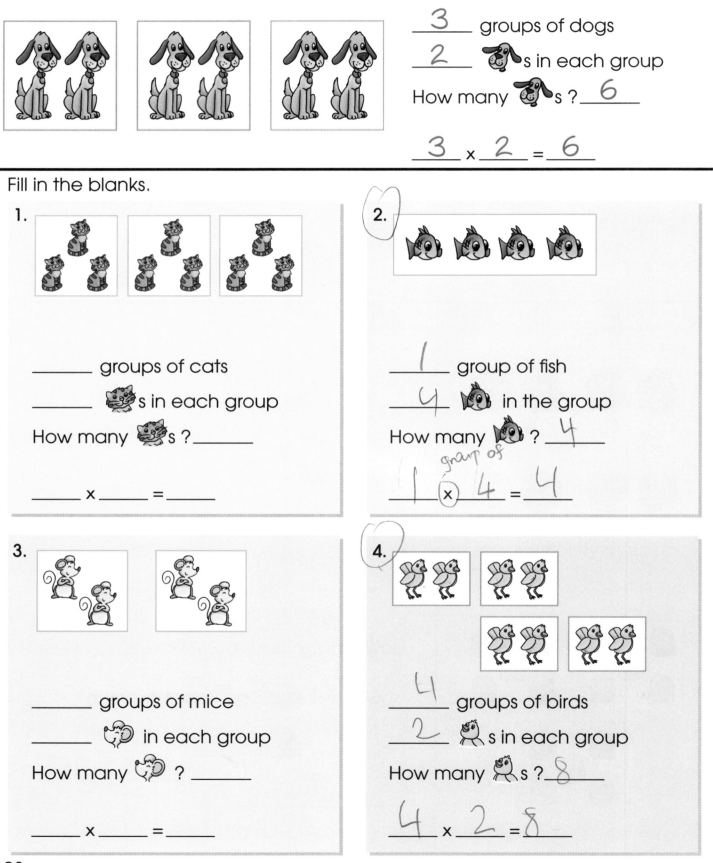 in each group

How many 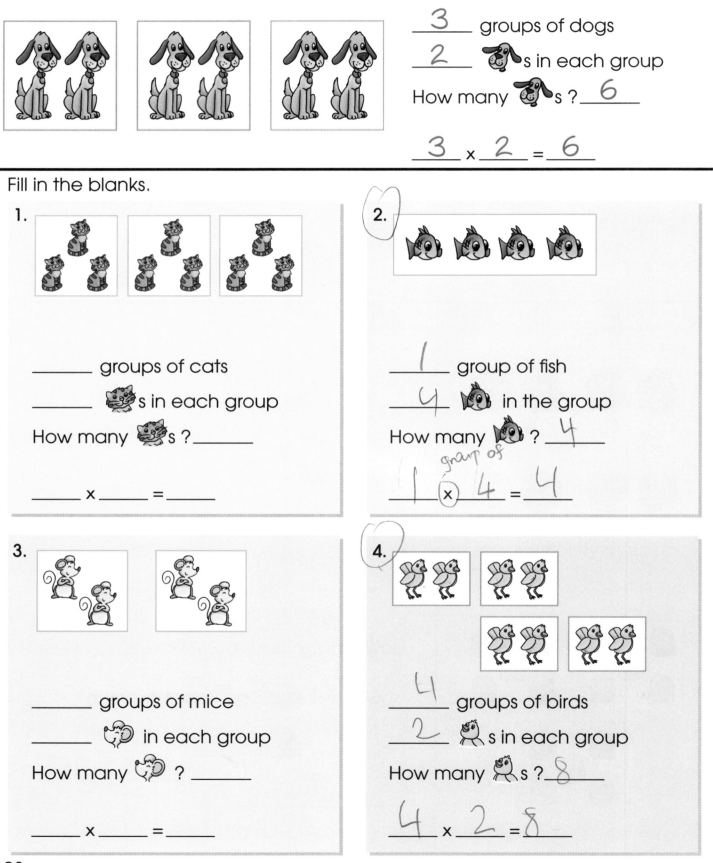 ? _____

_____ x _____ = _____

4.

____4____ groups of birds

____2____ 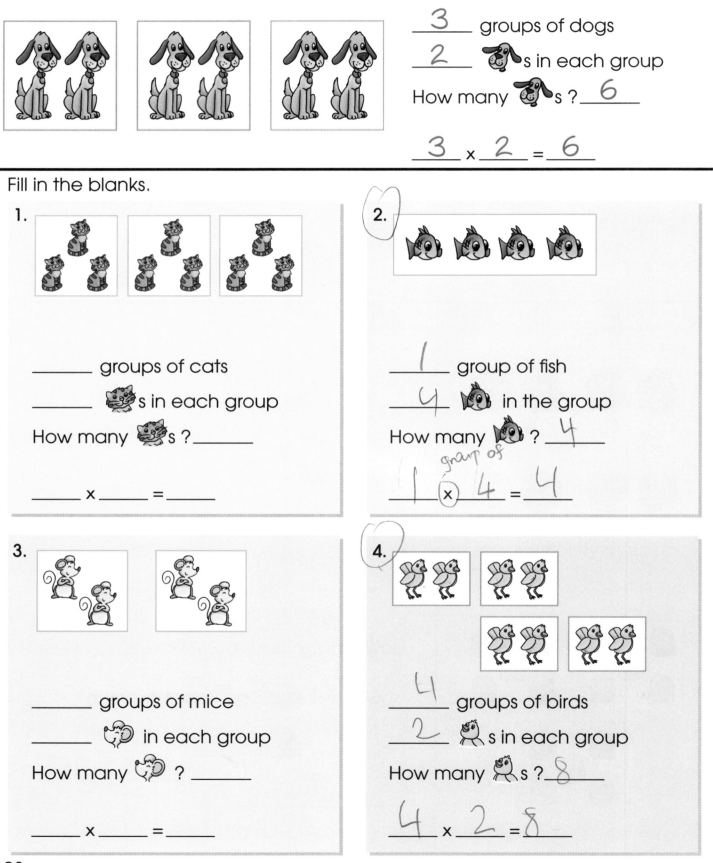s in each group

How many 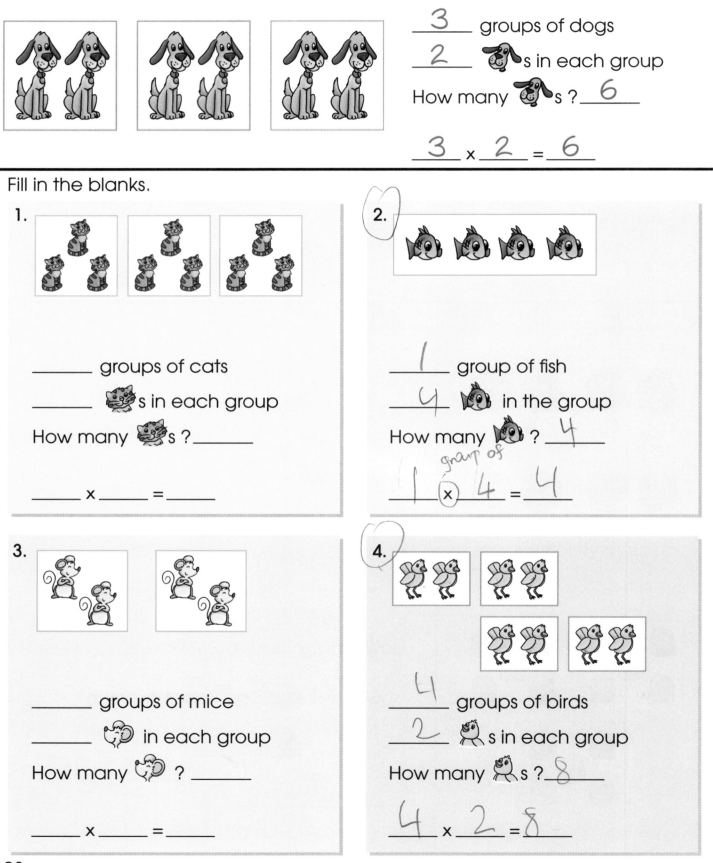s ? _8____

___4___ x ___2___ = _8___

© School Zone Publishing Company

Multiplication and Groups

Fill in the blanks.

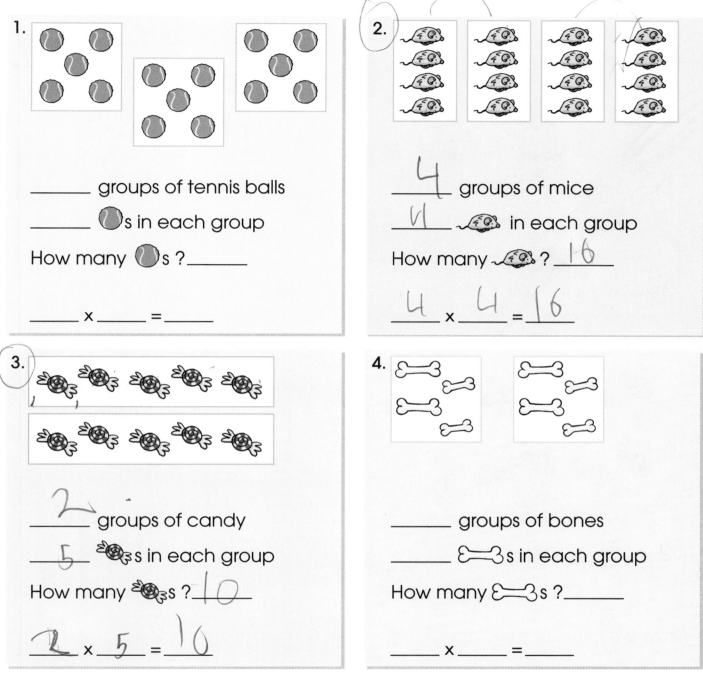

1.

_____ groups of tennis balls

_____ 🎾s in each group

How many 🎾s ? _____

_____ x _____ = _____

2.

__4__ groups of mice

__4__ 🐭 in each group

How many 🐭 ? __16__

__4__ x __4__ = __16__

3.

__2__ groups of candy

__5__ 🍬s in each group

How many 🍬s ? __10__

__2__ x __5__ = __10__

4.

_____ groups of bones

_____ 🦴s in each group

How many 🦴s ? _____

_____ x _____ = _____

5. Draw **2** groups of **3** eggs.

_____ x _____ = _____

6. Draw **3** groups of **3** snakes.

_____ x _____ = _____

Multiply by Two

Fill in the blanks.

1.

3 x 2 = _____

2.

2 x _____ = _____

3.

2 x _____ = _____

4.

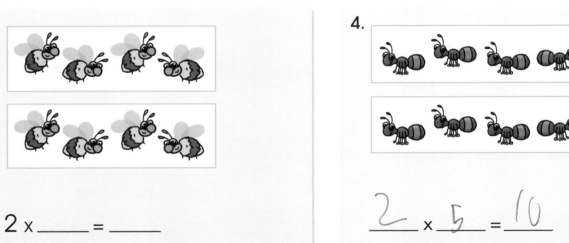

2 x 5 = 10

5. Draw **2** groups of **5** circles.

_____ x _____ = _____

6. Draw **4** groups of **2** squares.

_____ x _____ = _____

Multiply by Two and Three

The answer to a multiplication problem is called the **product**.

Find the **product**.

1. 2 x 3 = _____   2. 3 x 3 = _____

3. 3 x 5 = _____   4. 2 x 2 = _____

5. 2 x 4 = _____   6. 3 x 4 = _____

7. 3 x 1 = _____   8. 2 x 5 = _____

9. 3 x 0 = _____   10. 3 x 2 = _____

11. 2 x 1 = _____   12. 2 x 0 = _____

Fill in the chart.

x	0	1	2	3	4	5
2				6		
3	0				12	

Do you see any patterns?

Multiply by Four and Five

Find the **product**.

1. 4 x 2 = _____
2. 5 x 1 = _____
3. 5 x 3 = _____
4. 4 x 3 = _____
5. 4 x 4 = _____
6. 5 x 0 = _____
7. 4 x 1 = _____
8. 5 x 2 = _____
9. 5 x 4 = _____
10. 4 x 5 = _____
11. 4 x 0 = _____
12. 5 x 5 = _____

Fill in the chart.

x	0	1	2	3	4	5
2		2				
3						15
4	0			12		
5			10			

Do you see any patterns?

What I Learned about Numbers

Write the missing numbers.

1. 8, _____, _____, 11, _____, _____, 14, _____, 16, _____

2. 43, _____, 45, _____, 47, _____, 49, _____, _____, 52

3. 175, _____, _____, 178, _____, _____, 181, _____, _____, 184

4. 604, _____, _____, 607, _____, 609, _____, _____, 612

Which number comes **before**?

5. _____, 21, 22   6. _____, 57, 58   7. _____, 400, 401

8. _____, 99, 100   9. _____, 901, 902   10. _____, 555, 556

Which number belongs **between**?

11. 16, _____, 18   12. 39, _____, 41   13. 99, _____, 101

14. 138, _____, 140   15. 499, _____, 501   16. 888, _____, 890

What I Learned about Numbers

Which number comes **after**?

1. 18, 19, _____   2.   65, 66, _____   3.   47, 48, _____

4. 98, 99, _____   5. 308, 309, _____   6. 798, 799, _____

Circle the number that is **greater**.

7.   18   81   8.   60   16   9.   75   57

10.   183   138   11.   440   404   12.   693   637

Circle the number that is **less**.

13.   26   62   14.   70   79   15.   145   155

16.   372   327   17.   606   621   18.   565   556

19.   Circle the number that shows 4 tens.

354   453   345   435   534

20.   Circle the number that shows 5 hundreds.

354   453   345   435   534

What I Learned about Operations

Complete the **fact family**.

1. 4, 9, 13

____ + ____ = ____

____ + ____ = ____

____ - ____ = ____

____ - ____ = ____

2. 5, 7, 12

____ + ____ = ____

____ + ____ = ____

____ - ____ = ____

____ - ____ = ____

3. 7, 9, 16

____ + ____ = ____

____ + ____ = ____

____ - ____ = ____

____ - ____ = ____

Find the **sum**.

4.
```
  45
+ 32
```

5.
```
  63
+ 18
```

6.
```
  59
+  7
```

7.
```
  85
+ 69
```

8.
```
  37
+ 66
```

9.
```
  70
+ 59
```

10.
```
  345
+ 213
```

11.
```
  504
+ 235
```

12.
```
  342
+  57
```

13.
```
  325
+ 145
```

14.
```
  670
+  46
```

15.
```
  631
+  59
```

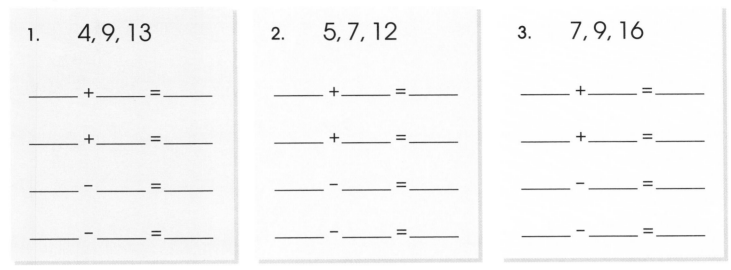

What I Learned about Operations

Find the **difference**.

1.
$$78 - 35$$

2.
$$45 - 9$$

3.
$$82 - 37$$

4.
$$58 - 20$$

5.
$$94 - 54$$

6.
$$67 - 63$$

7.
$$256 - 32$$

8.
$$567 - 234$$

9.
$$678 - 245$$

10.
$$482 - 56$$

11.
$$516 - 352$$

12.
$$674 - 655$$

Find the **sum** or **difference**.

13.
$$73 + 26$$

14.
$$87 - 46$$

15.
$$81 - 18$$

16.
$$281 + 18$$

17.
$$64 + 53$$

18.
$$349 - 47$$

19.
$$333 + 409$$

20.
$$376 - 208$$

Find the **product**.

21. $3 \times 4 =$ _____

22. $5 \times 2 =$ _____

23. $4 \times 1 =$ _____

24. $1 \times 5 =$ _____

25. $4 \times 5 =$ _____

26. $3 \times 0 =$ _____

What I Learned about Graphs

Use the pictograph to answer the questions.

1. Which snack is the favorite? _____

2. How many children like fruit as a snack? _____

3. More children like cookies than popcorn. How many more children like cookies?

    _____

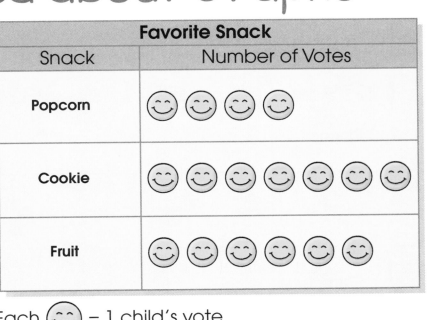

Favorite Snack	
Snack	Number of Votes
Popcorn	😊 😊 😊 😊
Cookie	😊 😊 😊 😊 😊 😊 😊
Fruit	😊 😊 😊 😊 😊 😊

Each 😊 = 1 child's vote

Use the bar graph to answer the questions.

4. How many children like cheese pizza? _____

5. Which pizza was the least favorite? _____

6. How many children like pepperoni pizza? _____

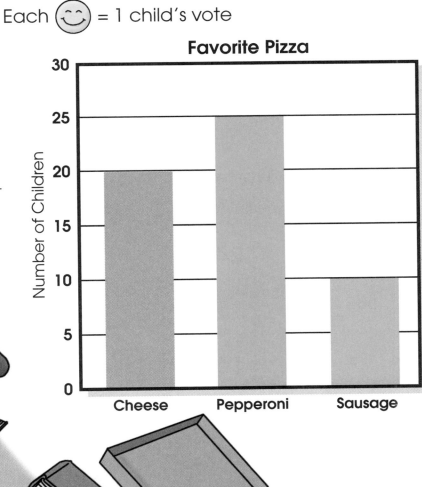

Favorite Pizza

What I Learned about Graphs

Use the groups of vegetables at the right to complete the tally chart.
Use the tally chart to answer the questions.

Vegetable	Tally	Total
Cabbage		
Carrot		
Corn		

1. How many carrots and ears of corn are there altogether? _____

2. There are more carrots than cabbages.
   How many more carrots are there? _____

Use the table to answer the questions.

Favorite Pet		
Pet	Girls' Votes	Boys' Votes
Cat	24	18
Dog	15	30
Bird	10	8

3. How many girls like cats? _____

4. How many boys like birds? _____

5. Which pet was the boys' favorite? _____

6. How many boys and girls like dogs? _____

Choose the Answer

Color in the oval of the correct answer.

1. 193 ◯ 139
   - ◯ <
   - ◯ >
   - ◯ =

2. 3 tens 4 ones ◯ 34
   - ◯ <
   - ◯ >
   - ◯ =

3. 192, _____ , 194
   - ◯ 93
   - ◯ 191
   - ◯ 192
   - ◯ 193

4. 300, 400, _____ , 600
   - ◯ 401
   - ◯ 410
   - ◯ 500
   - ◯ 550

5.
   - ◯ 130
   - ◯ 134
   - ◯ 140
   - ◯ 143

6. 643
   +226
   - ◯ 817
   - ◯ 823
   - ◯ 869
   - ◯ 879

7. 753
   -439
   - ◯ 313
   - ◯ 314
   - ◯ 315
   - ◯ 316

8.   5
   x 4
   - ◯ 9
   - ◯ 15
   - ◯ 20
   - ◯ 25

Answer Key

Page 1

1. 2, 5, 7, 9
2. 12, 14, 16, 18, 19
3. 8, 10, 11, 13, 15
4. 9, 7, 6, 4, 2, 1

Page 2

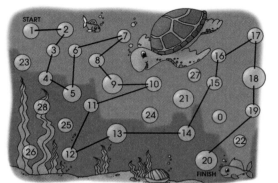

1. 7, 8, 9, 10, 11, 12
2. 11, 12, 13, 14, 15, 16
3. 15, 16, 17, 18, 19, 20

Page 3

1. 4   **2.** 8   **3.** 6
4. 2   **5.** 5   **6.** 10
7. 14   **8.** 16   **9.** 19
10. 7   **11.** 3   **12.** 8
13. 12 **14.** 10 **15.** 16
16. 14 **17.** 20 **18.** 18

Page 4

1. 5   **2.** 9   **3.** 13
4. 10   **5.** 17   **6.** 0
7. 5   **8.** 12   **9.** 17
10. 1   **11.** 18 **12.** 14
13. 5   **14.** 17 **15.** 20
16. 8   **17.** 19 **18.** 10

Page 5

1. 8   **2.** 14   **3.** 19
4. 10   **5.** 12   **6.** 18
7. 13   **8.** 15   **9.** 20
10. 7   **11.** 8   **12.** 2
13. 11 **14.** 13 **15.** 0
16. 9   **17.** 17 **18.** 12

Page 6

1. less   **2.** greater
3. greater   **4.** less
5. greater   **6.** greater
7. less   **8.** less
9. less   **10.** greater
11. 6
12. 9
13. Answers will vary;
        ≥ 8, 0-6

Page 7

1. 9   **2.** 7   **3.** 8
4. 8   **5.** 9   **6.** 10
7. 9   **8.** 10   **9.** 10
10. 10; 3 + 7 = 10

Page 8

1. 10   **2.** 10   **3.** 10
4. 2   **5.** 5   **6.** 7
7. Numbers circled in black.

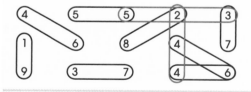

8. Numbers circled in red.

Page 9

1. 4   **2.** 6   **3.** 2
4. 5   **5.** 2   **6.** 6
7. 3   **8.** 5   **9.** 5
10. 5; 9 - 4 = 5

Page 10

1. 6 - 2 = 4   **2.** 7 - 3 = 4   **3.** 9 - 5 = 4
4. 8 - 3 = 5   **5.** 10 - 2 = 8   **6.** 9 - 6 = 3
7. 9 - 8 = 1   **8.** 10 - 5 = 5   **9.** 9 - 4 = 5
10. 10 - 4 = 6

Page 11

1. 12, 12, 7, 5
2. 10, 5
3. 3, 9, 6, 6
4. 6, 12
5. 11, 5, 5, 6
6. 4, 11, 7, 11

Page 13

1. 9   **2.** 3   **3.** 4   **4.** 4
5. 4   **6.** 7   **7.** 5   **8.** 7
9. 2   **10.** 8   **11.** 3   **12.** 6
13. 3   **14.** 3   **15.** 10 **16.** 10

Page 14

1. 4, 6   **2.** 6, 8   **3.** 9, 3
4. 6, 7   **5.** 7, 8   **6.** 9, 18
7. 4, 7   **8.** 7, 14   **9.** 9, 6
10. 6, 12 **11.** 9, 8   **12.** 5, 8

Page 12

1. 5 + 9 = 14   **2.** 9 + 6 = 15   **3.** 7 + 6 = 13
    9 + 5 = 14   6 + 9 = 15   6 + 7 = 13
    14 - 5 = 9   15 - 6 = 9   13 - 6 = 7
    14 - 9 = 5   15 - 9 = 6   13 - 7 = 6

4. 8 + 9 = 17   **5.** 8 + 6 = 14   **6.** 7 + 9 = 16
    9 + 8 = 17   6 + 8 = 14   9 + 7 = 16
    17 - 8 = 9   14 - 6 = 8   16 - 7 = 9
    17 - 9 = 8   14 - 8 = 6   16 - 9 = 7

Answer Key

Page 15

13, 12, 7
8, 13, 9
12, 9, 9
8, 14, 15
16, 17, 5
SECRETARY BIRD

Page 16

Set A has more correct answers.

Set A	Set B
15, 12	13, ~~14~~ (16)
6, ~~8~~ (9)	~~6~~ (7), 8
~~14~~ (15), 13	12, ~~13~~ (14)
9, ~~8~~ (9)	~~7~~ (8), 9

Page 17

1. 13 **2.** 17 **3.** 16 **4.** 14
5. 11 **6.** 18 **7.** 14 **8.** 15
9. 17 **10.** 12 **11.** 18 **12.** 16
13. 17 **14.** 12
15. 15 **16.** 18
17. 18 **18.** 20

Page 18

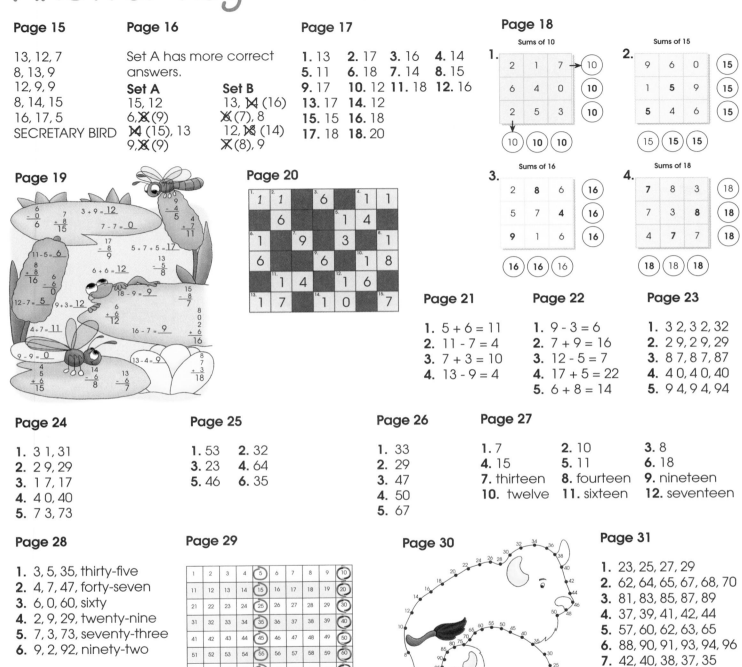

1. Sums of 10

2	1	7	→ 10
6	4	0	10
2	5	3	10
10	10	10	

2. Sums of 15

9	6	0	15
1	5	9	15
5	4	6	15
15	15	15	

3. Sums of 16

2	8	6	16
5	7	4	16
9	1	6	16
16	16	16	

4. Sums of 18

7	8	3	18
7	3	8	18
4	7	7	18
18	18	18	

Page 19

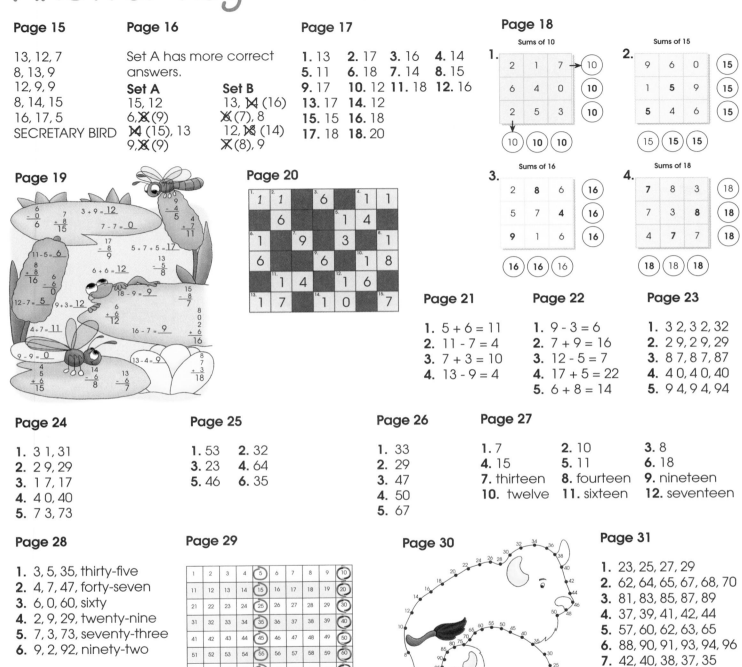

Page 20

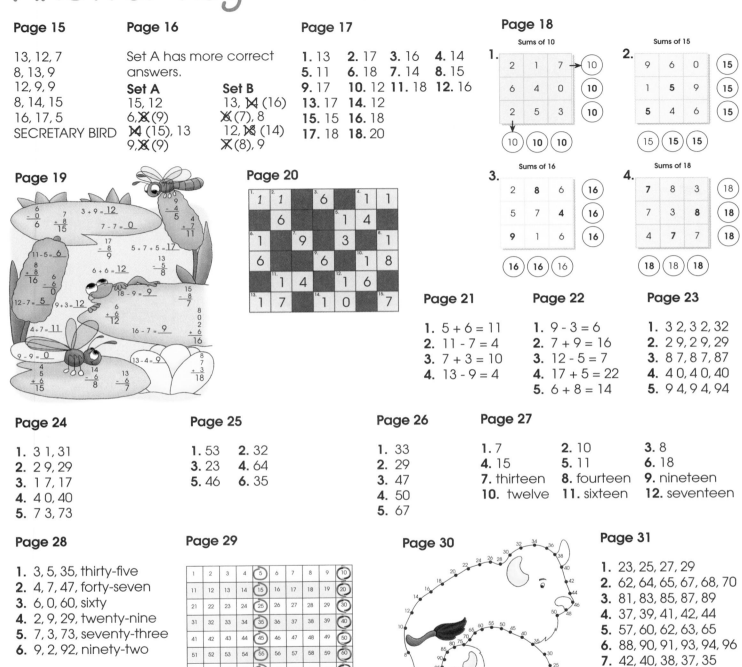

Page 21

1. 5 + 6 = 11
2. 11 - 7 = 4
3. 7 + 3 = 10
4. 13 - 9 = 4

Page 22

1. 9 - 3 = 6
2. 7 + 9 = 16
3. 12 - 5 = 7
4. 17 + 5 = 22
5. 6 + 8 = 14

Page 23

1. 3 2, 3 2, 32
2. 2 9, 2 9, 29
3. 8 7, 8 7, 87
4. 4 0, 4 0, 40
5. 9 4, 9 4, 94

Page 24

1. 3 1, 31
2. 2 9, 29
3. 1 7, 17
4. 4 0, 40
5. 7 3, 73

Page 25

1. 53 **2.** 32
3. 23 **4.** 64
5. 46 **6.** 35

Page 26

1. 33
2. 29
3. 47
4. 50
5. 67

Page 27

1. 7 **2.** 10 **3.** 8
4. 15 **5.** 11 **6.** 18
7. thirteen **8.** fourteen **9.** nineteen
10. twelve **11.** sixteen **12.** seventeen

Page 28

1. 3, 5, 35, thirty-five
2. 4, 7, 47, forty-seven
3. 6, 0, 60, sixty
4. 2, 9, 29, twenty-nine
5. 7, 3, 73, seventy-three
6. 9, 2, 92, ninety-two

Page 29

Page 30

Page 31

1. 23, 25, 27, 29
2. 62, 64, 65, 67, 68, 70
3. 81, 83, 85, 87, 89
4. 37, 39, 41, 42, 44
5. 57, 60, 62, 63, 65
6. 88, 90, 91, 93, 94, 96
7. 42, 40, 38, 37, 35
8. 74, 72, 70, 69, 67, 66

Page 32

1. 30, 50, 80
2. 15, 30, 40
3. 12, 18, 20, 24
4. 40, 60, 70, 90
5. 30, 40, 45, 60
6. 22, 24, 30, 32

Page 33

1. 52 **2.** 19 **3.** 44
4. 36 **5.** 87 **6.** 70
7. 99 **8.** 59 **9.** 78
10. 35 **11.** 47 **12.** 52
13. 50 **14.** 26 **15.** 74
16. 61 **17.** 83 **18.** 80

Page 34

1. 33 **2.** 39 **3.** 93
4. 70 **5.** 27 **6.** 51
7. 28 **8.** 62 **9.** 77
10. 41 **11.** 48 **12.** 70
13. 47 **14.** 83 **15.** 30
16. 68 **17.** 100 **18.** 39

Answer Key

Page 35
1. 63, 64
2. 57, 59
3. 16, 19, 61, 69
4. 83, 89, 93, 98
5. 53, 57
6. 53, 56, 63, 65

Page 36
1. 68   2. 84   3. 93
4. 70   5. 62   6. 88
7. 40   8. 90   9. 62
10. 77   11. 18   12. 20
13. 65   14. 43   15. 63
16. 91   17. 69   18. 28

Page 37
1. 26 < 35
2. 46 > 40
3. <   4. >   5. >
6. >   7. >   8. <
9. <   10. <   11. >

Page 38
1. 10, 12, 15
2. 36, 45, 49
3. 19, 25, 81
4. 18, 24, 36
5. 29, 41, 57
6. 30, 55, 72
7. 26, 56, 66
8. 72, 78, 87

Page 39
1. 4 2, 42
2. 3 9, 39
3. 6 0, 60
4. 5 3, 53
5. 7 8, 78
6. 9 4, 94

Page 40
1. 58   2. 42
3. 24   4. 91
5. 70   6. 85
7. 63   8. 36

Page 41
1. 43 > 34
2. 35 < 37
3. 58 = 58
4. 63 < 90

Page 42
1. >   2. <   3. <
4. =   5. >   6. >
7. >   8. <   9. >
10. >   11. <   12. >
13. >   14. =
15. >   16. =
17. 42

Page 43
1. 11, odd
2. 24, even
3. 33, odd

Page 44
1. 2, 4, 6, 8, 10, 12, 14, 16, 18, 20, 22, 24, 26, 28, 30, 32, 34, 36, 38, 40
2. 0, 2, 4, 6, 8
3. 1, 3, 5, 7, 9
4. odd   5. even   6. even
7. even   8. odd   9. odd
10. 6, 18, 64, 80, 58, 96
11. even; example: 2 + 4 = 6
12. even; example: 3 + 7 = 10
13. odd; example: 3 + 2 = 5
Examples may vary for 11–13.

Page 45
1. 2nd, 4th, 5th, 6th
2. eighth, ninth
3. 3rd, 5th
4. 3
5. Mike
6. Emma

Page 46
1. GRIN
2. TIME
3. LAND
4. CATS

Page 47
1. 34   2. 27   3. 48   4. 18
5. 58   6. 35   7. 68   8. 39
9. 19   10. 49   11. 87   12. 56
13. 77   14. 29   15. 99   16. 68

Page 48

1. 1	2. 9		3. 4	4. 6
5. 4	6. 3	7. 8	8. 5	9. 7
10. 3	11. 9	12. 7	13. 9	9
	14. 4	15. 9	16. 2	17. 8
18. 5		19. 2	20. 9	21. 3	22. 6
23. 8	24. 8		25. 4	26. 9
	9			8	

Page 49
1. 46   2. 69   3. 81   4. 87
5. 77   6. 86   7. 87   8. 48
9. 98   10. 69   11. 98   12. 66
13. 97   14. 99   15. 90   16. 99

Page 50

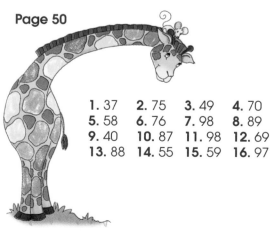

1. 37   2. 75   3. 49   4. 70
5. 58   6. 76   7. 98   8. 89
9. 40   10. 87   11. 98   12. 69
13. 88   14. 55   15. 59   16. 97

Answer Key

Page 51

Answers are clockwise from the arrow.
1. 50, 90, 70, 80, 60
2. 35, 40, 50, 60, 42
3. 88, 97, 76, 59, 69
4. 95, 83, 69, 80, 78

Page 52

1. 4	**2.** 43	**3.** 20	**4.** 7
5. 30	**6.** 8	**7.** 0	**8.** 10
9. 30	**10.** 11	**11.** 4	**12.** 80
13. 60	**14.** 41	**15.** 22	**16.** 60

Page 53

1. 2 tens 17 ones
   2 tens {1 ten 7 ones}
   → 3 tens 7 ones = 37
2. 6 tens 5 ones = 65
3. 8 tens 1 one = 81
4. 4 tens 9 ones = 49
5. 2 tens 6 ones = 26
6. 8 tens 0 ones = 80
7. 5 tens 9 ones = 59

Page 54

1. ⃝31	**2.** 39	**3.** ⃝50	**4.** 58
5. 59	**6.** ⃝81	**7.** ⃝80	**8.** 49
9. ⃝27	**10.** 89	**11.** ⃝80	**12.** ⃝45

Page 55

1. 52	**2.** 35	**3.** 82	**4.** 60
5. 60	**6.** 86	**7.** 61	**8.** 93
9. 50	**10.** 71	**11.** 91	**12.** 92

Page 56

1. 6	2. 4		3. 7	4. 8
5. 9	7		6. 8	4
7. 5	8. 9		9. 7	10. 3
11. 4	1		12. 3	8

Page 57

1. 32	**2.** 51	**3.** 61	**4.** 50
5. 43	**6.** 26	**7.** 93	**8.** 73
9. 84	**10.** 22	**11.** 67	**12.** 53

Page 58

1. 13	**2.** 26	**3.** 5	**4.** 57
5. 58	**6.** 19	**7.** 44	**8.** 18
9. 37	**10.** 11	**11.** 8	**12.** 0
13. 37	**14.** 24	**15.** 33	
16. 22	**17.** 13	**18.** 31	

Page 59

1. 33
2. 22
3. 50
4. 6
5. 51
6. 21

Page 60

Answers are clockwise from the arrow.
1. 31, 33, 22, 20
2. 35, 24, 32, 13
3. 55, 42, 36, 64
4. 22, 53, 25, 44

Page 61

1. 53 = 5 tens 3 ones
   → 4 tens 13 ones
2. 46 = 4 tens 6 ones
   → 3 tens 16 ones
3. 81 = 8 tens 1 one
   → 7 tens 11 ones
4. 39 = 3 tens 9 ones
   → 2 tens 19 ones
5. 92 = 9 tens 2 ones
   → 8 tens 12 ones
6. 13 = 1 ten 3 ones
   → 0 tens 13 ones
7. 60 = 6 tens
   → 5 tens 10 ones

Page 62

1. ⃝46	**2.** 33	**3.** ⃝89	**4.** 40
5. ⃝22	**6.** ⃝58	**7.** 51	**8.** ⃝14
9. ⃝38	**10.** 71	**11.** ⃝73	**12.** ⃝59

Page 63

1. 24	**2.** 56	**3.** 46	**4.** 11
5. 25	**6.** 28	**7.** 40	**8.** 39
9. 29	**10.** 64	**11.** 28	**12.** 18

Page 64

1. 2	2. 4			
3. 5	5			
		4. 4	5. 7	
		6. 1	6	
7. 3	8. 5			
9. 2	3			
		10. 6	11. 3	
		12. 3	9	

Page 65

1. 31	**2.** 47	**3.** 74	**4.** 28
5. 19	**6.** 85	**7.** 50	**8.** 90
9. 50	**10.** 18	**11.** 81	**12.** 10
13. 87	**14.** 30	**15.** 62	**16.** 2
17. 79	**18.** 69	**19.** 68	**20.** 69

Page 68

1. 37	**2.** eleven
3. 53	**4.** forty-eight
5. 68	**6.** 45 **7.** 70 **8.** 97
9. 36	**10.** 64 **11.** 45 **12.** 34
13. 87	**14.** 21 **15.** 49 **16.** 92

17.

Page 66

72, 67, 77, 81
64, 55, 19, 78
88, 55, 78, 53
19, 19, 66, 97
AFRICAN ELEPHANT

Page 67

1. 3 7, 37
2. 5 4, 54
3. 4 6, 46
4. 6 2, 62
5. 64 **6.** 80 **7.** 19
8. 40 **9.** 49 **10.** 100
11. < **12.** > **13.** <
14. 54, 60, 76

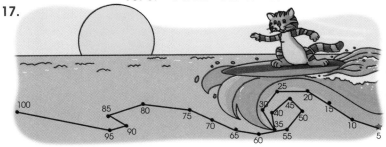

Answer Key

Page 69

1. ✝✝✝ ✝✝✝ ✝✝✝ ///; 18
2. 20
3. 22
4. hamburgers
5. 20 + 18 = 38
6. 22 - 18 = 4
7. 22 + 18 + 20 = 60

Page 70

Bird Color		
Color	Tally	Total
Blue	✝✝✝ ✝✝✝ //	12
Brown	✝✝✝ ✝✝✝	10
Red	✝✝✝ ////	9

1. blue
2. 10 + 9 = 19
3. 12 - 9 = 3
4. 12 + 10 + 9 = 31

Page 71

Number of Flowers		
Type of Flower	Tally	Total
Daisy	✝✝✝ ✝✝✝ ✝✝✝ ✝✝✝ ✝✝✝ /	26
Rose	✝✝✝ ✝✝✝ ✝✝✝ ✝✝✝ ✝✝✝ ✝✝✝ /	31
Tulip	✝✝✝ ///	8
Sunflower	✝✝✝ ✝✝✝ ✝✝✝	15

1. tulips
2. 26 + 15 = 41
3. 31 - 8 = 23
4. 26 + 31 + 8 + 15 = 80

Page 72

Baseball Card Collections		
Name	Tally	Total
John	✝✝✝ ✝✝✝ ✝✝✝ ✝✝✝ //	22
Alan	✝✝✝ ✝✝✝ ✝✝✝	15
Nick	✝✝✝ ✝✝✝ ✝✝✝ ✝✝✝ ✝✝✝	25
Jason	✝✝✝ ✝✝✝ ✝✝✝ ////	19

15, 25, Nick, 40, 6, 81

Page 73

1. 6
2. 12
3. 8
4. cartoons
5. 12 - 6 = 6
6. 12 + 8 = 20
7. 12 + 6 + 8 = 26

Page 74

1. 11
2. 12
3. 12
4. 14
5. Jim
6. Dan, Megan
7. 14 + 12 = 26

Page 75

1. 4, 6, 8, 10
2. 10
3. 8
4. 4
5. 12 - 6 = 6
6. Count by twos.

Page 76

1. 5 books
2. Count by fives.
3. 20
4. 25
5. Justin
6. 15 + 35 = 50
7. 35 - 25 = 10
8. 15 + 25 + 35 + 20 = 95

Page 77

1. 2 stamps
2. Count by twos.
3. 18
4. 16
5. Lisa
6. Ray
7. 20 - 16 = 4

Page 78

1. 6
2. 7
3. 9
4. summer
5. winter
6. 11 - 7 = 4

Page 79

1. 8
2. 9
3. 6
4. Maria
5. Brad
6. Kim, Jay
7. 6 + 8 + 9 + 8 = 31

Page 80

1. 12
2. 14
3. orange, 18
4. grape, 10
5. 18 - 12 = 6
6. 14 + 10 = 24
7. more than 50
   14 + 18 + 10 + 12 = 54

Page 81

1. 20
2. 25
3. 30
4. ice cream, 35
5. 35 - 20 = 15
6. 20 + 35 = 55

Page 82

1. 25
2. 40
3. grade 3, 45
4. 20 + 25 = 45
5. 45 - 20 = 25
6. less than 50
   20 + 25 = 45

Page 83

1. 15
2. 10
3. 17
4. blue
5. purple
6. 20 + 15 = 35
7. 17 - 10 = 7

Page 84

1. 40
2. 38
3. 22
4. 32
5. summer
6. winter

Answer Key

Page 85

1. 4 hundreds = 400
2. 6 hundreds = 600
3. 8 hundreds = 800
4. 5 hundreds = 500

Page 86

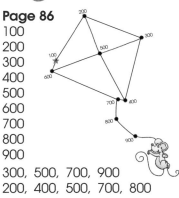

100
200
300
400
500
600
700
800
900

300, 500, 700, 900
200, 400, 500, 700, 800

Page 87

1. 3 hundreds 7 tens 4 ones
   374
2. 2 hundreds 5 tens 9 ones
   259
3. 4 hundreds 5 tens 0 ones
   450
4. 6 hundreds 0 tens 4 ones
   604

Page 88

1. 253 2. 325

3. 532 4. 235

5. 352 6. 523

Page 89

1. 422
2. 280
3. 800
4. 512
5. 180
6. 966
7. 324
8. 678
9. 700
10. 555
11. 90
12. 944

13. 2, 5, 8, 25, 28,
    52, 58, 82, 85,
    258, 285, 528,
    582, 825, 852

Page 90

1. 487
2. 289
3. 333
4. 825
5. 400
6. 899
7. 215
8. 458
9. 570
10. 867
11. 648
12. 444
13. 796

Page 91

Page 92

1. 102, 104
2. 216, 218, 220
3. 747, 750
4. 515, 525, 530
5. 400, 500, 700
6. 420, 440, 460
7. 650, 665, 670

Page 93

1. 344 2. 800 3. 613
4. 110 5. 728 6. 499
7. 164 8. 412 9. 317
10. 241 11. 180 12. 300
13. 135 14. 717 15. 206
16. 651 17. 390 18. 600

Page 94

1. 221 < 223
2. 167 < 207
3. 246 = 246
4. 203 < 230
5. < 6. > 7. <
8. < 9. < 10. <

Page 95

1. 368 2. 584 3. 903
4. 700 5. 262 6. 878
7. 640 8. 910 9. 565
10. 770 11. 418 12. 532
13. 765 14. 943 15. 639
16. 391 17. 609 18. 728

Page 96

1. 327, 329, 392
2. 107, 170, 701
3. 355, 535, 553
4. 617, 618, 671
5. 432, 434, 437
6. 264, 273, 282
7. 191, 901, 911
8. 489, 490, 498
9. 839, 858, 883
10. 319, 351, 393

Page 97

1. 117 2. 109 3. 132 4. 121
5. 107 6. 110 7. 100 8. 150
9. 136 10. 176 11. 110 12. 111
13. 143 14. 121 15. 132 16. 120

Page 98

1. 68 2. 119 3. 104 4. 294
5. 59 6. 120 7. 149 8. 123
9. 99 10. 197
11. 168 12. 84
13. 88 14. 220
15. 146 16. 160
17. 404

Page 99

1. 783 2. 838 3. 659 4. 579
5. 494 6. 881 7. 607 8. 568
9. 483 10. 862 11. 715 12. 796
13. 521 14. 610 15. 800 16. 801

Answer Key

Page 100

1. 198 **2.** 267 **3.** 886 **4.** 246
5. 451 **6.** 117 **7.** 362 **8.** 264
9. 532 **10.** 172 **11.** 775 **12.** 375
13. 595 **14.** 485 **15.** 481 **16.** 683

Page 101

1. 623
2. 43
3. 526
4. 312
5. 535
6. 222

Page 102

1. 124 **2.** 801 **3.** 412 **4.** 321
5. 350 **6.** 330 **7.** 61 **8.** 504
9. 458 **10.** 431 **11.** 207 **12.** 623
13. 723 **14.** 117 **15.** 148 **16.** 412

Page 103

220, 61, 474
67, 724, 206
328, 759, 675
657, 580, 878
A BLUE BIRD

Page 104

1. 1	2. 2	3. 1		4. 2	5. 7	6. 1
	7. 7	0	6		8. 4	3
9. 6	8	9			4	5
5			10. 7	11. 4		
12. 4	7	0		13. 9	1	3

Page 105

1. 4 + 4 = 8
2 groups of 4 = 8
2 x 4 = 8
2. 2 + 2 + 2 + 2 = 8
4 groups of 2 = 8
4 x 2 = 8
3. 5 + 5 + 5 = 15
3 groups of 5 = 15
3 x 5 = 15
4. 1 + 1 + 1 + 1 = 4
4 groups of 1 = 4
4 x 1 = 4

Page 106

1. 8, 4 x 2 = 8
2. 12, 4 x 3 = 12
3. 25, 5 x 5 = 25
4. 12, 3 x 4 = 12
5. 5, 5 x 1 = 5
6. 15, 3 x 5 = 15
7. 9, 3 x 3 = 9
8. 16, 4 x 4 = 16

Page 107

1. 4
2
8
4 x 2 = 8
2. 3
5
15
3 x 5 = 15

Page 108

1. 3 groups
3 in each group
9
3 x 3 = 9

2. 1 group
4 in the group
4
1 x 4 = 4

3. 2 groups
2 in each group
4
2 x 2 = 4

4. 4 groups
2 in each group
8
4 x 2 = 8

Page 109

1. 3 groups
5 in each group
15
3 x 5 = 15

2. 4 groups
4 in each group
16
4 x 4 = 16

3. 2 groups
5 in each group
10
2 x 5 = 10

4. 2 groups
4 in each group
8
2 x 4 = 8

5. 2 groups of 3 eggs

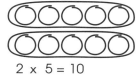

2 x 3 = 6

6. 3 groups of 3 snakes

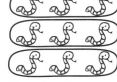

3 x 3 = 9

Page 110

1. 3 x 2 = 6
2. 2 x 2 = 4
3. 2 x 4 = 8
4. 2 x 5 = 10
5. 2 groups of 5 circles

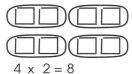

2 x 5 = 10

6. 4 groups of 2 squares

2 x 5 = 10

4 x 2 = 8

Answer Key

Page 111

1. 6   2. 9
3. 15   4. 4
5. 8   6. 12
7. 3   8. 10
9. 0   10. 6
11. 2   12. 0

X	0	1	2	3	4	5
2	0	2	4	6	8	10
3	0	3	6	9	12	15

Each column goes up
by the row number.

Page 112

1. 8   2. 5
3. 15   4. 12
5. 16   6. 0
7. 4   8. 10
9. 20   10. 20
11. 0   12. 25

X	0	1	2	3	4	5
2	0	2	4	6	8	10
3	0	3	6	9	12	15
4	0	4	8	12	16	20
5	0	5	10	15	20	25

Each column goes up
by the row number.

Page 113

1. 9, 10, 12, 13, 15, 17
2. 44, 46, 48, 50, 51
3. 176, 177, 179, 180, 182, 183
4. 605, 606, 608, 610, 611
5. 20   6. 56   7. 399
8. 98   9. 900   10. 554
11. 17   12. 40   13. 100
14. 139   15. 500   16. 889

Page 114

1. 20   2. 67   3. 49
4. 100   5. 310   6. 800
7. 81   8. 60   9. 75
10. 183   11. 440   12. 693
13. 26   14. 70   15. 145
16. 327   17. 606   18. 556
19. 345
20. 534

Page 115

1. 4 + 9 = 13   2. 5 + 7 = 12
   9 + 4 = 13   7 + 5 = 12
   13 - 4 = 9   12 - 5 = 7
   13 - 9 = 4   12 - 7 = 5

3. 7 + 9 = 16   4. 77   5. 81   6. 66   7. 154
   9 + 7 = 16   8. 103   9. 129   10. 558   11. 739
   16 - 7 = 9   12. 399   13. 470   14. 716   15. 690
   16 - 9 = 7

Page 116

1. 43   2. 36   3. 45   4. 38
5. 40   6. 4   7. 224   8. 333
9. 433   10. 426   11. 164   12. 19
13. 99   14. 41   15. 63   16. 299
17. 117   18. 302   19. 742   20. 168
21. 12   22. 10   23. 4
24. 5   25. 20   26. 0

Page 117

1. cookie
2. 6
3. 7 - 4 = 3
4. 20
5. sausage
6. 25

Page 118

Vegetable	Tally	Total
Cabbage		6
Carrot		12
Corn		8

1. 12 + 8 = 20
2. 12 - 6 = 6
3. 24
4. 8
5. dog
6. 30 + 15 = 45

Page 119

1. >
2. =
3. 193
4. 500
5. 134
6. 869
7. 314
8. 20

AWARD

Great Job!

_____

First Name

_____

Last Name

finished Math Basics 2
from
School Zone Interactive.